The excitement of prayer brought to life!

[*Kit Cat and the Whirling Watches*] is a wonderful presentation to give children a knowledge of our biblical heritage. It gives them tools to help them participate in preserving our religious liberty.

Vonette Bright
Co-chairman, National Day of Prayer

The book was interesting and funny and cool.

Andy, age 12

Kit Cat and the Whirling Watches is an intriguing story that I believe will hold grade schoolers (and Mom's and Dad's, too) spellbound as the story of America's National Day of Prayer unfolds. I believe it's never too early to establish in the minds of America's younger generation the priceless spiritual heritage we have in our nation and how only the prayers of God's people can sufficiently guard that heritage for generations to come.

Dick Eastman
President, Every Home for Christ
Chairman, America's National Prayer Committee

I enjoyed this book and expect to use the prayer guide.

Rebecca, age 11

The excitement of prayer is brought to life in *Kit Cat and the Whirling Watches*. A great curriculum tool to highlight the National Day of Prayer for both private and public school educators!

Judy Turpen, National Prayer Coordinator
Christian Educators Association Int'l

Prayer can be fun...

What a delight to have Kit Cat show us one of the bright sides of America! Prayer can be fun, it can be exciting, and it can turn our nation to God. This is a vital book for our new generation.

C. Peter Wagner
President, Global Harvest Ministries

[*Kit Cat and the Whirling Watches*] was used during a study of American History. It greatly enhanced our study.

Mrs. Schulder, Home-school mom

I thought the book was great. I felt as if I was part of [Miss Baker's fifth grade] class.

Cynthia, age 13

[*Kit Cat and the Whirling Watches*] will be so important in the days to come to preserve in the minds and hearts of children the true history of our nation and the vital part prayer has played.

Lin Story,
National Children's Prayer Network

I found the book remarkably creative and very informative. The prayer guide is a great idea.

Mrs. Vernon, 6th grade teacher

Kit Cat and the Whirling Watches is a unique, imaginative, and well-written book which will help many children understand what a Day of Prayer is. Parents and children alike will enjoy the fast-moving, interesting tale. Best of all, this book properly used will help children pray meaningfully for their friends and their country. I know of no other book which give parents and children this kind of help.

Alvin J. Vander Griend
Minister of Evangelism Resources
Christian Reformed Church

Kit·Cat

and the
Whirling
Watches

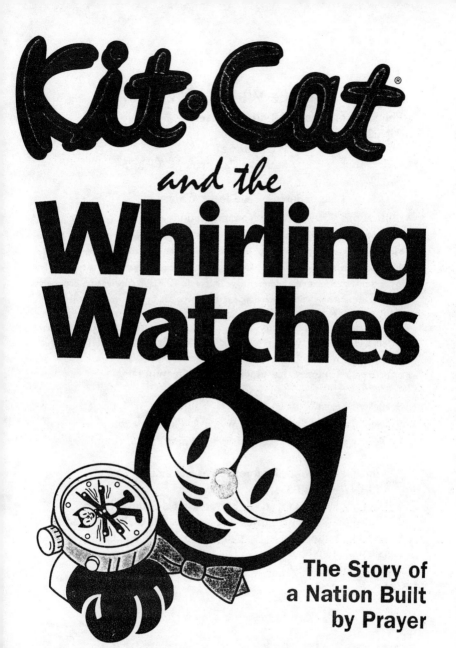

**The Story of
a Nation Built
by Prayer**

SUSAN SORENSEN
& JOETTE WHIMS

Kit-Cat® and the Whirling Watches:
The Story of a Nation Built by Prayer
Published by: Joy Publishing
                     P.O. Box 827
                     San Juan Capistrano, CA 92675

Text ©1994 Susan Sorensen and Joette Whims
Illustrations ©1994 Woody Young Creations

Illustration Design: Woody Young   Illustration Artist: Craig White
Cover: David Marty Design   Cover Coordinator: Michelle Treiber

Library of Congress Cataloging-in-Publication Data

Sorensen, Susan.
    Kit-Cat® and the Whirling Watches: The Story of a Nation Built by Prayer / Susan Sorensen and Joette Whims.
          p.   cm.
    Includes bibliographical references and index.
    ISBN 0-939513-33-1 :
1. National Day of Prayer. 2. Prayer--United States--History.
3. United States--Religious life and customs. 4. Children's stories, American. 5. Religion in the public schools--United States--Law and legislation. I. Whims, Joette. II. Title. III. Young, Woody
BL2525.S583   1994   93-41627
291.4'3'0973--dc20   CIP

All Scripture is taken from the *New International Version*.

Kit-Cat® is a registered trademark of California Clock Company and is used with permission.

Printed in the United States of America.   98 97 96 95 94 - 10 9 8 7 6 5 4 3 2 1

Contents

To Vonette Bright and the National Prayer Committee
who revived a national tradition of prayer.

To the many men, women and children who pray
tirelessly for this nation and its leaders. As Paul
Billheimer beautifully stated it:

When the books are opened
and the spiritual history of the nation is unfolded,
it will be written for all to read
*that the **pray-ers**,*
not the mayors, kings, prime ministers,
presidents or presidents' men,
are the real molders of events.

Dear Parents and Teachers:

A s Americans, we have been given a precious treasure in our national, spiritual heritage. Part of this richness includes a designated day to unite in bringing our petitions and thanksgiving to God on behalf of our country. That day is called the National Day of Prayer.

As we look back at the tradition of prayer in our nation's history, we see that prayer has played an important part in the development and growth of our nation. President George Bush said in his National Day of Prayer Proclamation in 1989:

> *The great faith that led our Nation's Founding Fathers to pursue this bold experiment in self-government has sustained us in uncertain and perilous times; it has given us strength and inspiration to this very day. Like them, we do very well to recall our "firm reliance on the protection of Divine Providence," to give thanks for the freedom and prosperity this Nation enjoys, and to pray for continued help and guidance from our wise and loving Creator.*
>
> *Our challenge is to pass this tradition of prayer on to the next generation. They have a young faith and a vision to change our nation for good. We can tap into that great resource by teaching them to pray for their country as well.*

But some may have questions about the advisability of bringing our religious heritage into the classroom. Educators and administrators in the past few years have come to agree that the typical response to the Supreme Court decisions abolishing state-mandated prayer and devotional use of the Bible in the public schools was to completely ignore the rich spiritual heritage of our nation. This has led to an imbalance in our schools. Albert Shanker, President of the American Federation of Teachers, wrote in 1990:

> *If students don't know anything about the religions that helped shape our cultural heritage, they'll have a very limited appreciation of that heritage...Fortunately, people of all political and religious persuasions now agree that it's important to introduce teaching about religion into the curriculum.[1]*

We agree! In trying to fill part of the need to inform our children, we wrote *Kit Cat and the Whirling Watches* specifically about the rich heritage of prayer in our nation and the ongoing practice of prayer by our Congress, presidents and local governmental leaders. We were also concerned that, as the National Day of Prayer began to show up on calendars, parents and teachers had a resource to educate children about this commemorative day as they did other national observances.

The adventures of Kit Cat and Miss Baker's class draws heavily from historical information and current observances of the National Day of Prayer. We have documented many of the references to actual quotes and congressional proceedings in the Endnotes. You will also find a number of historical documents and proclamations at the back of the book.

If possible, read *Kit Cat and the Whirling Watches* with your children or students so you can discuss themes and information. Encourage children to create their own "hands-on" prayer guide by following the instructions in the "Your Prayer Guide" section. Use the proclamations by Presidents Washington, Lincoln and Bush to discuss why our presidents proclaim a day of prayer. Show the children how to research information about leaders and issues in our government so that they can pray more specifically. By doing this, children will not only become better citizens, but they will be a part of impacting our country's future for the good!

A number of products for your home or classroom are available through the National Day of Prayer Task Force. The address is: P.O. Box 15616, Colorado Springs, CO 80935-5616. Or call: (719)531-3379. For a minimal cost you can order posters, bookmarks and prayer guides. A prayer calendar, *My Family's Prayer Calendar,* is available to help your family pray for your country. It contains practical suggestions for remembering national and local needs throughout the year. The Task Force can inform you of observances in your area.

A National Children's Prayer Network exists to teach and motivate children to pray for this nation. For more information, you can write: Lin Story, The National Children's Prayer Network, P.O. Box 9683, Washington, D.C., 20016. Or call: (703)759-3778.

The following is a list of ideas you can use at home or in your classroom. Adapt them for your situation:

Parents:

- Develop a family prayer guide. Use pictures of government leaders, a map of the United States, newspaper clippings, and the encyclopedia to help your children pray specifically.

- Develop a practice of praying with your children for current events or for the areas outlined in the prayer guide. Concentrate on issues that concern you as a family.

- Look up all references to "prayer" in the Bible. Discuss how you can use these verses to pray effectively for the areas listed in your prayer guide.

- Put a prayer bulletin board in an obvious place in your home. Tack up pictures or articles on issues that concern you in our country. Discuss and pray for the events as a family. Allow your children to have their own opinions. Include exciting events as well as national crises or disturbing trends.

- Invite your children's friends or neighbors to make prayer guides with you and show them how to pray for their country. Include their parents when possible.

- Take a trip around your city. Follow the plan in Joshua 6, driving around the city once a day for six days, then seven times on the seventh day. Stop often to pray for things you observe. Plan and write down ways to put your prayers into action in your city and neighborhood and follow through on your plans.

- Encourage relatives and friends to help your family observe the National Day of Prayer in your area. Order brochures from the National Day of Prayer Task Force before May to give to your friends. Find out what is being offered in your area and attend one of the local observances together.

Teachers:

- Have your class write to the White House requesting the National Day of Prayer Proclamation for the current year. Read through the proclamation with your students and discuss the themes and any new or difficult words.

- Set up a prayer file of 3x5 cards with specific names and concerns for which to pray. Make up a card for each of your national, state, county and city leaders. Your local library can help you research these leaders' names. Record prayer requests under each name. Include appropriate Bible verses. Use the prayer file throughout the year.

- Assign your students an essay like Miss Baker's class wrote or ask them to draft their own National Day of Prayer Proclamation. Or write an opinion essay on how our country would be different without our religious heritage. Display their work on the week of the National Day of Prayer.

- Lead a classroom discussion considering why our presidents proclaim days of prayer urging the nation to give thanks to God. Discuss how our country would be different if we did not have our heritage of thanking God.

- Role play one historical event in the National Day of Prayer such as the signing of the NDP bill. Take a field trip to your state capital or local observances of the National Day of Prayer. You can find out what is happening in your area by writing the NDP Task Force.

- Create a time-line of all the historical events in *Kit Cat and the Whirling Watches*. Under each date, record pertinent facts about that time in history.

- Create a class prayer guide. Have each student or small group adopt a local government leader, a person in need or someone who serves other people in your area who they can contact for prayer requests. Collect newspaper articles and information about each person or group.

- Write the President or any of your national or state representatives for an 8x10 photograph. Display it in your classroom, then let those leaders know you are praying for them.

- During the week of the National Day of Prayer, take each day to pray for the categories listed in the prayer guide. Divide the prayer requests from Saturday and Sunday throughout the school week. If possible, plan to help those in need or encourage the Christian media and other groups to pray. Discuss how to pray for families and school authorities.

- Read the First Amendment and discuss the meaning of separation of church and state.

- Study the process of a bill becoming law. Assign oral reports on the parts of this process.

- Make a prayer map. Have your students bring in articles about current events that concern them and attach the articles to the map at the places where the events occurred. Do this all year. Take down the article when God answers the prayer.

For more information on ways you can creatively introduce our religious heritage into the classroom, write:
Christian Educators Assoc. Int'l
P.O. Box 50025
Pasadena, CA 91115-0025
(818) 798-1124

The Kit Cat Klock

You probably think nothing surprising or unusual could ever happen in an ordinary classroom. That's what the students in Miss Baker's class thought, too. But were they ever wrong!

Miss Baker's students were proud of their classroom. It had big, airy windows and soft-green walls. Miss Baker was one of the best teachers to have in fifth grade. She had a way of making boring subjects come alive and difficult lessons easy to understand. Sometimes she was serious, but other times she surprised everyone by doing things on the spur of the moment. When she peered through her glasses and had that funny grin on her face, her students knew something was up.

Everyone at Valley Elementary School stopped by to check out the new things Miss Baker put in her room. This month she had a real wasp's nest in a jar, a Handy Talkie radio, and several bright dragon kites from China. Even so, most school days came and went pretty much the same for her fifth graders.

But things were about to change. One day Miss Baker bought an old clock at a garage sale. It was a

13

black-and-white Kit Cat Klock with a tail that wagged and eyes that rolled. She cleaned it up and discovered that it kept perfect time.

Miss Baker took down the plain grey clock that had hung above the chalkboard longer than even Principal McDonald could remember and put the Kit Cat Klock in its place. The students were delighted. But none of them had any idea how much that clock would change the routine in their classroom.

1

Whirling Watches

The day didn't start out too well in Miss Baker's fifth grade class. After taking attendance, she had her students gather at the work tables. Then she announced an essay contest.

"Oh, no! Not an essay contest!" Marvin moaned. He shoved his hand through his dark, curly hair in frustration. He hated anything to do with writing. Sammy, who was sitting next to Marvin, buried his head in his arms.

Miss Baker handed a few fliers to George, Mary and Laura. "Wait a minute, Marvin," she said. "There's more to it than that. Our radio station, KXYZ, is sponsoring a contest to promote the National Day of Prayer."

"The what?" blond, petite Elizabeth asked. "I've never heard of that." She shoved two fliers to Tony who quickly gave one to Scott.

"I know what it is," Scott announced. "My dad is promoting the contest at the station. He says *every* American should know about this day on our calendar."

Mary gave Julie a knowing look and tossed extra fliers to her. Ben grabbed three from Julie and passed one to Jose and to Oknah.

Miss Baker handed Marvin a couple of fliers. He acted like they were hot potatoes. Bouncing the last one on his fingertips, he gave it to Sammy.

Miss Baker opened the pamphlet. "To enter," she explained, "we have to write on the topic, 'Prayer in Our Nation.' KXYZ is sponsoring the contest for the National Day of Prayer in May."

"I hate essays," Marvin blurted.

Scott laughed. "If the whole class has to work on it, we can get Laura to do the writing. She wants to be a reporter."

Laura's face turned almost as red as her auburn hair, blotting out her freckles. "Thanks a lot," she said.

Miss Baker raised her hand. "Just a minute. Let's read the flier." She scanned the first page. "The essay can be no more than 2,000 words and no less than 1,000. But it has to be completed in two months. That doesn't give us much time."

She looked up. "We'll need something special to make our entry unique. Lots of sharp classes will be entering. I talked to teachers from Roosevelt and Central schools. They're really excited about the project." Her brown eyes studied her students. "The essay that wins will have to stand out. Any ideas?"

The classroom fell silent. The Kit Cat Klock above the chalkboard seemed to tick especially loudly as Miss Baker waited for an answer.

"What's the prize?" Jose asked.

"Look at the bottom of the second page," Miss Baker said. The students looked at their fliers. "Fifth prize is a $50 gift certificate for books for our library."

"Laura would like that," Elizabeth teased. "Her mom's the high school librarian."

Laura blushed.

"Fourth prize is $200 worth of software for our computer," Miss Baker explained.

"All right!" Scott broke in. "Let's order Super Mario Brothers."

"I'm sure they mean educational games," Elizabeth informed him curtly.

Miss Baker waited for the room to quiet. Then she announced in that tone she used when she considered something very important, "The three top prize-winning classes get to attend a specialbrunch in the governor's mansion."

"Ooo," Oknah sighed, "I've never been in a mansion before."

"Neither have I," Mary agreed. "But I have been to the Capitol building. It's so big inside, my voice sounded like an echo."

"We could make it a full day's field trip," the teacher went on explaining. "We'd tour the Capitol grounds and meet the governor and his wife. Winning classes could come from other cities, too, since this is a statewide contest."

A crease crossed her forehead. "The decision is yours. Let's take a vote. How many of you would like the class to enter?"

Mary's and George's hands shot up. Oknah raised hers timidly.

Sammy shook his head. He didn't like anything that wasn't a sport or a motor. "National Day of Prayer? Sounds boring to me."

"Yeah," Elizabeth chimed in.

"Well, maybe," Mary retorted. "But I want to go on a field trip." She was always eager to try something new.

Ben, who was quite cautious, admitted, "That might be fun."

"Then you write the essay," Marvin suggested.

"No, I don't want to do that. Guess it isn't a good idea." Ben slipped his flier into his math book.

George and Marvin began arguing about the contest. Oknah, who sat between them, scrunched her head down to avoid the words flying back and forth. Mary tried to convince Julie and Elizabeth to change their votes. Jose, Scott and Tony jumped into the discussion, too. The voices in the room rose higher and higher.

Suddenly, a smooth, silky voice commanded, "Stop!"

The room was instantly silent. The students looked around to see where the strange voice had come from.

"Who said that?" Laura whispered to Mary.

Mary shrugged.

The only movement in the classroom came from the tail on the Kit Cat Klock above the board. It seemed to stop ticking, then twitched once, twice, three times. The wide eyes flipped from side to side as if they were scanning the room.

No one moved. The only sounds were the ticking of the clock and the gentle flutter of leaf mobiles hanging from the ceiling.

Suddenly, with a swoop of black fur and the plop of padded paws, a cat hopped out of the clock and onto the floor.

The class gasped. Miss Baker whirled around.

The cat beamed a wide half-moon smile. "Hey, kids. What's the fuss about?"

No one said a word.

The thick, black whiskers swished as the cats face slipped into a sly grin. "Cat got your tongues?" he chuckled.

Miss Baker finally moved. She cautiously stepped up to the cat and stroked his head with one finger. "Are you real?" she asked.

The cat laughed, his low voice bubbling in his throat and ending in a purr. "Of course, I'm real." He bowed. "I'm Kit Cat. Feel that sleek fur?" He rubbed his elbow over her hand.

"Well, I never!" Miss Baker exclaimed as she looked him over from head to toe.

Paws on his hips, Kit Cat asked. "What's this I hear about a contest?"

No one answered for a minute. Then Marvin piped up, "It's a stupid essay contest."

"About the National Day of Prayer?" Kit Cat asked.

"Yeah," Julie and Tony answered at the same time.

"Sounds like fun. Want some help with the research?"

The students looked at each other.

"Miss Baker, if you don't mind," Kit Cat said as he bowed again.

She nodded weakly.

Kit Cat reached into some secret pocket-place in his furry coat and brought out a handful of wrist watches. With a mischievous sparkle in his eye, he padded up and down the rows, handing one to each student. Each person cautiously took the watch he offered them.

When he got back to the front, he walked up to the teacher. "I have one for you, too." He gave her the last one.

"What is this?" she asked as she examined the watch. It had a white dial with red numbers. Kit Cat's picture filled the center, and the hour and minute hands looked like cat's paws.

"It's a special piece of equipment," Kit Cat explained. "It can take us to many places. Try it on."

Miss Baker strapped it to her wrist. It fit perfectly.

"How does it work?" Sammy asked as he put his watch to his ear.

"Who can say?" Kit Cat purred mysteriously. "Would you like to travel to the past to see how prayer has influenced the United States?"

Mary bounced in her seat. "Like time travel?"

"You bet," Kit Cat said.

Miss Baker frowned. "I don't know."

"It's completely safe, ma'am," Kit Cat said in his silky tone.

Miss Baker got that funny grin on her face. "Well, this can't be real, so why not."

"Where do you want to go first?"

Sammy brightened. "Let's go back to the first Thanksgiving. Turkey is my favorite food. I'm hungry."

"Great idea!" Kit Cat smiled. "We'll stop at several places. Hang on to your hats." Before Miss Baker could say a word, he pressed the stem on his watch, and the hands began to turn in the wrong direction.

A gentle rumble spread throughout the room as the hands on the other watches started circling backwards, too. Faster and faster they went until the paw-hands became flashing black streaks.

The objects in the room began to fade into a rainbow of pastel colors. Oknah grabbed Mary's hand, and Tony took in a long, loud breath.

A fresh breeze with the smell of wind-swept prairie, rain-washed forest, and blooming desert all mixed in a delightful bouquet swirled past. Then a feeling like the drop of a fast elevator lurched everyone's stomach.

Suddenly, the class found itself knee-deep in the grass of a bright meadow. A wide patch of newly-cut tree stumps lined the edge of the forest nearby.

"Students," Kit Cat announced grandly, "welcome to Plymouth, Massachusetts."

Whiz. Thud. A flying arrow narrowly missed Sammy's ear and drove deeply into a nearby tree trunk.

"Watch out!" Sammy shouted as he dove to the ground.

Another speeding arrow shot past Miss Baker's skirt. The rest of the students and the teacher threw themselves flat as a cluster of arrows whistled past.

"What have we gotten ourselves into?" Marvin muttered to Ben whose white face was pressed to the ground next to his.

Ben shrugged, his face blank with fear.

2
Campfires and Musket Guns

Several loud shots ripped the air, and musket balls spun over the students' heads. A line of men in odd clothing and stiff hats were pointing long-barreled guns directly toward Miss Baker's class. Five or six Indians dressed in deerskin aprons and moccasins formed a second line to the right. They were pulling back on bow strings.

Elizabeth noticed Kit Cat still standing. "Get down," she hissed, "they're shooting at us!"

Kit Cat laughed. His chuckle floated oddly in the dangerous meadow. "Don't worry," he said. "No one can see you or hear you or even touch you."

Marvin's head popped up. "Really?"

Kit Cat helped Miss Baker up. Then he pointed. "See those markers? That's what they're shooting at. The Pilgrims and Indians are having a marksmanship contest. They don't even know we're here."

One-by-one, the students got to their feet. Laura was the last to stand. "What if you're wrong?" she asked timidly.

Kit Cat put his arm around her. "It's fine." He motioned to the class. "C'mon." He led them across the meadow and onto a dirt road which wound up a hill.

As they walked, Laura pulled out a small notebook and pencil she had slipped into her pocket before they left the classroom. She poised her pencil. "When was the first Thanksgiving?"

"Probably in October. In the year 1621. Right after the harvest." Kit Cat responded.

Laura scribbled a few lines in her notebook. "Where was it held?"

"Plymouth, Massachusetts. Where we're standing right now."

The group topped the hill and gazed down into a valley where a tiny town nestled. Eleven one-room houses built of sawed pine boards with thatched roofs and four larger buildings were huddled together on both sides of the road. Small harvested fields dotted the hills behind the crude buildings.

Kit Cat and the rest made their way to town and walked through the main street.

"That's the Common House," Kit Cat said as they stopped in front of the largest building. "It's filled with corn, pumpkins and squash."

Farther on, Miss Baker and her students saw planks set on sawhorses serving as picnic tables. Handmade stools were scattered around the tables and grass. Clusters of Pilgrim men and Indians mingled while women in long skirts and white linen caps tended the many blazing campfires. Boys in knee-high pants and girls in long dresses with white aprons were helping with the preparations.

One Indian wore a single feather tucked into a high crest of hair running from the front of his head to the back. Scott pointed. "Who's that?"

"Squanto," Kit Cat explained. "He was a special friend of the Pilgrims. He taught them how to plant corn, squash and pumpkins, how to fish, and which wild herbs and berries to eat."

"I've heard of him before," Laura said. She went back to her notebook. "Who all was at that first Thanksgiving?"

"Actually," Miss Baker said in her teacher-voice, "the Pilgrims invited the Indians because the settlers knew they wouldn't have survived the first winter without their native American friends."

"Right," Kit Cat agreed. "Four white men went 'fowling' with their musket guns and brought back wild turkeys, geese and ducks to last a week." He pointed to a gun leaning against a stump. "This is what their guns looked like. Pretty primitive compared to the hunting rifles in the stores of our day, huh?"

The fifth graders nodded.

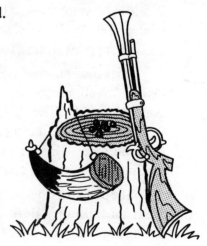

"Chief Massasoit and ninety of his tribe came for the feast. They brought five deer to add to the cooking fires."

"Wow! What a lot of food!" Sammy exclaimed.

Scott inspected the old gun without touching it. It looked well-used but carefully oiled and cleaned. When he looked up, the others had continued on down the road. He loped to catch up with them.

Another meadow spread evenly on the other side of town. Several foot races were in progress. Two Indians were wrestling inside a circle of on-lookers. A short, squat man looked like the underdog. Suddenly, with a quick move, he overpowered his opponent and proudly stood to his feet. Muscles rippled under his tawny skin.

"Where's the *Mayflower*?" Ben asked as he noticed water sparkling through the trees down the road.

"Went back to England last spring," Kit Cat explained. "What a life-saver that it didn't leave earlier. That first winter was so hard, the *Mayflower* became their hospital ship."

Kit Cat tipped back his head and closed his eyes as if he could see the scene. "The Pilgrims arrived in the New World in November—too late to plant crops or prepare for winter. Their ship was so crowded, they didn't bring enough supplies to last."

Miss Baker moved aside as the wrestlers passed right by her. "Well, pardon me," she joked. When they were gone, she said, "The Pilgrims came to find a place to worship freely. All during the long, perilous sea journey, they believed their hardships were God's way of testing their faith and courage."

She paused as the foot racers brushed by her, too, then went on talking, "Before they landed, the Pilgrims drafted and signed the *Mayflower Compact*. It was a promise, under God, to set up an orderly government. When they reached land, they knelt to thank God for a safe crossing."

"Why didn't they celebrate Thanksgiving right then?" Mary asked with a frown crinkling her forehead. "Why did they wait a whole year?"

"Winter was coming." Kit Cat explained. "First they built the Common House, then they began erecting one-room houses.

"Just imagine! There were less than a hundred people. Some had died on the sea voyage. All they could see was wilderness. They were afraid of the Indians.

"Sickness began to strike. First they turned the Common House into a hospital. When it was full, they used the *Mayflower*. Those who were well cared for the sick. That left fewer men to build their homes."

Kit Cat led them up Leyden Street to a well-tended cemetery on a large hill. Neat wooden grave-markers stood in straight rows. "In the hardest part of the winter, two to three people died in a single day. Half the Pilgrims died that terrible winter."

Oknah gently touched the wooden marker near a tiny mound. "This must be a child's grave," she said.

Kit Cat stopped in front of the largest marker. "When spring came, everyone worked in the fields, even the sick." He pointed to the grave. "Governor Carver died one day while working alongside everyone else. Still the Pilgrims believed that God loved them."

Oknah's eyes filled with tears. "What faith!"

The group left the cemetery and began to make their way back to town.

When they reached the Common House, the crude tables were piled with roasted birds, shucked corn and golden pumpkins. Black pots bubbled over the softly glowing embers.

"Too bad we can't try out the food," Sammy said as the class gazed at the feast before them.

Just then Squanto and a short, red-haired man came striding up. "A beautiful day, Miles," Squanto declared.

"That's Miles Standish," Kit Cat whispered. "Some call him Captain Shrimp behind his back. You can tell by his clothes that he's not a Pilgrim. They hired him in England to train them to defend themselves. Now he's the go-between for the colonists and Indians."

"Oh, the smell of a bubbling pot over a well-laid fire," Miles sighed. "Who could ask for more?" He eyed the hot corn bread one of the women set on the table.

A tall, stately man with long curly hair and a stiff beard gave a shout.

"That's William Bradford, the new governor," Kit Cat explained.

Pilgrims and Indians gathered around the tables. A hush settled over the crowd.

William Bradford stood on a small rise. "Our barns are full," he said in a dignified voice. "Our homes have been built." He bowed toward the Indians beside him. "We have made excellent friends." He looked up into the sky. "We have come to this remote part of the world for the glory of God and the advancement of the Christian faith."[1] He looked over the crowd. "Let us thank God for the bounty of this land."

Men, women and children bowed their heads. The governor prayed in a low, rich voice. When he finished, the people sat down at the tables and on the grass.

Kit Cat led the class back the way they had come. Little puffs of dust rose from their feet as they walked up the road. The sounds of chattering birds and the wind sighing fell softly on their ears.

Suddenly Laura whispered, "That's it!" She turned to Jose. "I've got it. Thank God for the bounty of our land. That's the perfect topic for our essay." She scribbled on her tablet.

When they reached the meadow, George asked, "How are we going to get back?"

"Yeah," the other students echoed.

Kit Cat smiled and lifted up his watch. "No time to get back. We've got more stops to make first."

Miss Baker braced herself. Her students did, too. None of them were quite sure what would happen next.

Kit Cat twitched his tail, and the hands on the watches began to fly forward...

3
Just in Time!

A split second after Kit Cat twitched his tail, Miss Baker's class found itself in a high-ceilinged room filled with men wearing knickers and wigs with curls. Three lit candles in tall holders stood in a row down the middle of a long table. The men were staring at an official-looking document resting on the table.

"Who on earth are these guys?" Tony asked Kit Cat.

"We're in the State House—now called Independence Hall—in Philadelphia, Pennsylvania," Kit Cat explained. "These men are the Continental Congress. They're the ones who helped form our nation. It's 1775. One year before the Declaration of Independence was signed."

Kit Cat pointed out several men. "That's Sam Adams, and that's John Hancock, president of the Congress. Over there is John Jay, and that's Ben Franklin."

"Wow!" Ben exclaimed, excited about seeing such a famous person with his name.

The children quieted when one of the distinguished men began to speak. "John," Sam Adams, a man with serious eyes, said, "what should we do to set the dignity of this observance?"

John Hancock looked around at the other men. "Let's walk to Christ Church as a group to pray."

"Yes," John Adams agreed. "Since we requested every inhabitant of the English colonies dedicate this day for prayer and fasting, we must unite in prayer as well."

He placed his fists firmly on the table, rocking the candle near his hand. "I have received many reports that our proclaimed Day of Prayer is well received. Right now, thousands of colonists are fasting from sunrise to sunset from Georgia to New Hampshire. Colonists are going to their own houses of worship to pray, including the Jewish synagogues."

John Jay walked to the window and looked out. "We

have so much to ask God for." He looked back at his friends. "Our people are scattered all over the colonies. We need to be united into one people."

The rest nodded solemnly.

Mr. Jay faced the group and frowned deeply. "Georgia is the only colony that has not sent delegates to the Continental Congress. We must ask God to unite all the colonies in this righteous cause."

Ben Franklin, with his little pince-nez glasses and his weathered face, straightened the front of his coat jacket. "General George Washington has issued an order directing his troops to observe the fast. If our soldiers are fasting and praying in their humble lodgings, we can do no less." He walked toward the door. "Truly, our first order of business as a Congress is to ask the protection and guidance of Almighty God."

The men prepared to leave.

"Why are they so determined to pray?" Elizabeth asked.

Kit Cat's face became serious. "They're under threat of death. They're leading the revolution against the British army. If they're captured, they'll be hung. They know the English army could destroy this newly-forming country, especially if the colonists squabble with each other. That's why they called for a Day of Prayer."

The men of the Continental Congress went out the door. When the room was empty, the children ran up to look at the document on the table. It had IN CONGRESS

printed in large letters at the top. At the bottom of the page
was John Hancock's impressive signature.

"Wow," Scott breathed. "Look at this." He read
from the paper:

> This Congress, therefore, considering the present
> critical, alarming and calamitous State of these Colo-
> nies, do earnestly recommend, that THURSDAY, the
> Twentieth Day of July next, be observed by the
> INHABITANTS of all the English Colonies, on this
> Continent, as a Day of public HUMILIATION, FAST-
> ING, and PRAYER, that we may, with united Hearts
> and Voices, unfeignedly confess and deplore our
> many Sins, and offer up our joint Supplications to the
> All-wise, Omnipotent and Merciful Disposer of all
> Events.[1]

Miss Baker lightly touched the parchment. "Amazing!"

Kit Cat motioned. They followed him outside.

The dignified group of statesmen were already on the
street slowly walking the four blocks to Christ Church.
Their chins were firm and their eyes solemn. People
passing by stopped to watch. Kit Cat and his friends
brought up the rear, unnoticed.

When they reached Christ Church, the men entered
the lofty sanctuary and took places at the front. The wood
from the pews gleamed in the glowing candlelight. Kit Cat
and the fifth grade class slipped into the back.

Reverend Mr. Duche, chaplain of the Continental
Congress and an Anglican clergyman, took his place

behind the pulpit and spoke from the fourteenth chapter of the Psalms. He called his sermon "The American Vine." His low, rich voice exclaimed, "Return, we beseech thee O God of Hosts! Look down from Heaven and behold and visit this Vine!"[2]

After finishing his sermon, the minister prayed for the colonies and the Continental Congress. He asked forgiveness for the sins of the people.

The air hung richly with reverence and humility. Even the slightly damp smell of the church building deepened the feeling of holiness.

When the service ended, the Congressmen left the church and walked back to the State House to continue their work. Their unseen visitors followed them back.

After the men had taken seats around the long table, a messenger barged into the room. "This has arrived from Georgia," he said.

John Hancock opened the letter. He read it silently, then announced, "Georgia has joined the American cause!"

The men cheered. Although no one could hear them, the children shouted, too.

Sam Adams' face beamed. "This was one of the blessings we asked God to give us. He has already rewarded our prayers."

Without another word, the men bowed to thank God. When they finished, Kit Cat led his group outside. He pointed. "In that direction is the First Presbyterian Church. The Continental Congress will pray there tonight. The men of the Congress are from many different churches, but they want to create unity by worshipping together—no matter which church they attend."

"Wow, I never knew that." Mary took one more look at the brown-and-white State House standing grandly behind her. "Was that the only time they prayed?"

Kit Cat shook his head. "Oh, no. This Day of Prayer was the first of more than a hundred fifty days of prayer or thanksgiving proclaimed during our national history. A few years later, the delegates of the Constitutional Convention met to write the Constitution. These men asked God's guidance to help them draft a strong document to run the country, too."

Kit Cat pointed back at the State House. "They pounded out the language for the Constitution in that same building. At first, the delegates couldn't agree on what to include in the document. Many argued that the states should have the greatest power. Others insisted that the federal government should be strongest."

Kit Cat shook his head. "You'd think the delegates would be so excited about starting a new country that they would get along."

He closed his eyes as if he could see the scene. "One day in 1787, the delegates just couldn't agree. Arguments flew around the room. A few delegates left the State House in disgust. It looked as if the Constitutional Convention would break up."

"What happened?" Oknah asked.

"Benjamin Franklin stood to his feet. He was almost eighty—the oldest person there and respected by everyone. He pleaded with the delegates to take the matter to God in prayer."

Miss Baker's face lit up. "I read his speech in the material I collected for our essay." She concentrated for a moment. "It starts: `In the beginning of the contest with Britain...'" She stopped because she couldn't remember the rest.

Kit Cat straightened his bow tie and finished the quote:

"...when we were sensible of danger, we had daily prayers in this room for Divine protection...And have we now forgotten this powerful Friend? Or do we imagine we no longer need His assistance?

I therefore beg leave to move that, henceforth, prayers imploring the assistance of Heaven and its blessing on our deliberation be held in their assembly before we proceed to business."[3]

"What happened?" Ben asked.

"When they began working on the Constitution again a few days later, attitudes started to change. The call for prayer began to unify the delegates—just in time."

Looking up at the State House, Ben whispered, "Think of all the history that happened in this place. It's amazing!"

The others students nodded.

"It is awesome," Marvin said.

Laura scribbled furiously in her notebook.

"Yeah, all the history," Jose echoed.

Then, before anyone could say another word, Kit Cat twitched his tail and their watches began whirling again...

4

Cannon Fire in the Woods

With a bump, the fifth graders found themselves in a large meadow ringed by dark trees. Laura murmured, "I feel something cold and wet on my legs."

Feeling a draft, George wrapped his arms around himself.

A gentleman was kneeling in the snow in front of them. He wore a dark coat and white pants. He raised his

41

hands, then folded them in prayer. His big grey horse waited patiently near him.

Marvin burst out, "We're in the snow! We're really here! We're at Valley Forge and that's George Washington."

"Right on!" Kit Cat exclaimed.

Sammy stood up straighter. "I dont believe it. The first President of the United States!"

Kit Cat pointed past the dark trees in front of them. "Valley Forge is that way. George Washington has slipped off alone to pray. He isn't president yet, but he is Commander-in-Chief of the American armies."

With a spray of snow, a soldier riding a horse bolted through the clearing. Forgetting he was invisible, Sammy dived into a snow bank to avoid the flying hoofs.

The soldier pulled up next to George Washington. "We need you back in camp, sir. The battle's beginning again."

General Washington mounted his horse. He and the soldier swiftly rode back to camp. Kit Cat followed their trail on foot. The class straggled along behind him, plowing their way through the powdery snow.

They soon found themselves in a camp made of twelve-man log huts chinked with mud.

"It looks like a movie set!" Jose shrieked.

Tony picked up a stick and challenged Sammy to a duel. Sammy grabbed a longer stick and they faced off. Laughing, they lunged at each other.

Two men, one wearing rags on his feet and the other in worn, holey boots, carried a homemade stretcher down the foot-tramped path. A soldier with crude bandages wrapped over his chest lay on the stretcher. His face looked as white as the snow. Real blood oozed through the white wrappings.

When they saw the wounded soldier, Tony and Sammy stood still, then dropped their sticks. The men carried the stretcher to one of the huts and disappeared inside.

Gaunt, ragged soldiers shuffled through the camp in rows of four. A bitter wind picked up which made the men hunch in their thin clothing.

Cannon fire shook the woods. Laura ducked as if the cannon balls were flying right by her head.

Kit Cat led them to a hut a little larger than the other buildings. They ducked in the door.

General Washington was inside, giving orders to an aide. His face looked careworn and sad in the flickering candlelight.

"I know provisions are severely depleted," he said. "Several states have refused to send the supplies they promised to provide. I sent a message to Congress but they don't believe how serious our situation is. Every morning, more men take to their beds because of sickness. Cornwallis is just waiting for spring to arrive. I'm sure he thinks we'll have no strength left to fight by then."

The aide, holding his three-cornered hat in hand, merely nodded.

The Commander-in-Chief sighed. "Only God can help us now. I have spent most of the night in prayer for my men. Naked and starving as they are, we cannot enough admire the incomparable patience and fidelity of these soldiers.[1] I believe God will give us the victory."

The aide shuffled his feet.

"Go tell the officers that we will have a meeting right away."

The aide left. General Washington bowed his head. His lips moved in prayer, but no words could be heard.

The invisible group slipped out of the hut. They didn't say a word until they had left the camp behind.

"What happened to those men?" Jose asked.

"Somehow they survived the winter," Miss Baker answered, "George Washington had 11,000 soldiers. He lost two thousand men during skirmishes and to illness that winter.

"But the American army came out strong and hardened that spring. Some say that the hardships of that winter made the difference in the victory. That's why the winter of Valley Forge is called the 'Crucible of Freedom.' After that winter, General Washington defeated Cornwallis at Yorktown."

"Wow," Jose sighed.

The group started walking through the woods again. "The colonists were so impressed with George Washington's leadership," Kit Cat explained, "that many wanted to make him king. George Washington refused. Having a king would only make the new nation's government just like the countries they had left."

"It would be hard to turn down a king-job," Marvin said.

"But just think how different our country would be today if we had a king." Julie said.

The others murmured, "Yeah."

Kit Cat announced, "We have more things to see this morning." He calmly gathered everyone around him. "Here we go."

By now, the children knew what to expect.

"Where are we going next?" Scott asked.

Before he could get an answer, the watches began whirling once more...

5

The Darkest Days

One lone black man sat on an old log, head in his hands. He wore brown pants held up by suspenders and a pressed, white shirt buttoned all the way to his neck. He had hung his soft wool hat on his knee.

To his left, a huge crowd ringed a platform where a man spoke in a loud voice. His listeners all wore black and seemed wrapped up in what he said. To the right, a large roped-off herd of horses stamped and snorted and munched the stiff fall grass.

Kit Cat led his friends around the edge of the herd. "We're at Gettysburg, Pennsylvania," he said. "It's the middle of the Civil War. November of 1863." He led his group near the log.

A man in the navy-blue uniform of a Union soldier on a home made crutch limped up. He wore a dusty navy-blue cap with a shiny brim. The chin strap hung from one side. "Well, William Slade," he said as he stuck out his hand.

"John. John Burke," William said as he shook the man's hand. He patted the log beside him. "Take a load off your feet. It's been a long time since we chewed the rag."

John sat. His straggly mustache bristled under his sharp nose. "Yep, I been busy," he said. "Picked up this here bad knee in the Battle of Gettysburg. Lucky I wasn't hit worse."

"I heard the fighting was hot as the inside of a brick oven," William said.

John leaned forward. "Yeah, we were marched up in a hurry on the second of July. The fighting had already gotten heavy. I heard there was skirmishes going on at Cemetery Hill. Seemed like there was battle lines everywhere."

William's smooth forehead wrinkled. "Confederate Army was doing something. We saw hundreds of Federal soldiers retreating through town that day."

John nodded. "Things did look bad. We were sent to Seminary Ridge. Our eighty cannons faced the Confederates. They had twice that many pointed at us.

The next day round one o'clock, the big guns started firing.

"You can't imagine the noise. So loud it was like a roar. Iron death rained down around us. Smoke was blowing everywhere. The smell was so thick, I thought I would choke.

"The cannons fired for two hours. Seemed like an eternity. Us foot soldiers stood behind the guns and waited."

John grimaced. "Then the Confederate assault began. I watched the troops move through their guns and begin marching across the field toward us. They walked in total silence. Thousands of them half a mile long. Man touching man, grim as death and in perfect order."

John shivered. "Didn't seem like anything could stop those grey lines. We started shooting. I reloaded my carbine as fast as I could. That's when I took the hit in my knee. I could tell it wasn't bad, but I couldn't stand."

John rested his crutch on his good leg and hung his hat over the cross piece. "So many soldiers were wounded. One group was so close, I could hear their commander scream, 'Come on boys. Give them cold steel.' "

"When the Confederate soldiers reached our lines, we fought hand-to-hand. I just prayed they wouldn't get as far as me."

"Did they?" William asked.

"No. Our men broke their ranks before they

reached the wall." For a moment John just looked at the dark stripe running down the side of his blue pant leg. Then he continued. "After the Confederates retreated, the field was covered with dead and wounded. Groans and cries came from everywhere."

Neither man spoke for a couple minutes. Then the crowd applauded something the speaker had said. John nodded toward the distant platform. "Mr. Everett's been talking for more than an hour."

"Yep," William said. "Probably will go on for some time yet. I'm just waiting for President Lincoln to say his piece."

John wiped off his worn, dusty boots with his hand. "Why the President? Everett's the best speaker around. There's twenty thousand people who showed up to hear him."

William put his hat on and wrapped his hands around one knee. "Since President Lincoln got off the train last night, I been waiting on his needs."

"For sure!" John exclaimed.

"I've heard an ear-full since then. There's more important people in the Will's house than I can name." He slapped his cap against his pants. "Everyone's stamping and prancing around like restless cattle. There's not enough places to bed them all down. Some's sleeping in chairs in the parlor."

"You don't say."

William put on his important look. "Early this

morning, I brought a carriage around for the President. He went out to look at the battle sights. When he came back, he had the saddest look on his face." William's voice caught as if he were going to cry. Embarrassed, he stood and began walking away. John hobbled to catch up.

Kit Cat and the class followed a few steps behind.

"What'd you hear?" John prodded.

William didn't answer until they came to a huge stack of new, wooden coffins piled on the ground. He pointed. "See those?"

Fresh mounds of new graves lay in neat rows almost as far as they could see.

"Yeah."

"There's more dead soldiers to bury than we got coffins. They wanted to get them all put down before today's ceremony. But the train brings in more all the time."

"Those are all new graves?" John asked in a hushed voice. "How many died?"

"Fifty thousand soldiers and five thousand horses and mules. Union soldiers, Confederate prisoners, and towns people tried to bury everything as fast as they could. They burned the animal carcasses. And the flies! They covered everything."

William puffed up his chest. "David Wills owns the largest house on the town square. He bought seventeen acres for the cemetery. It was his idea to dedicate the ground. They all wanted Everett to speak. President Lincoln was asked as kind of an after-thought."

William took off his hat again. "I was listening to the President's secretary last night in Mr. Will's parlor. Mr. Hay says the President's heart is heavy. 'Specially right after the Second Battle of the Bull Run. Every time the list of the dead comes in, he reads every name. He prays for hours for the fighting to stop. He says he won't let our country break up. But he sure won't let slavery go on either."

"Some say he's not a God-fearing man," John said. "Some say he doesn't even believe in God."

"Don't you believe it!" William exclaimed. "Don't you remember the President called for a day of prayer and fasting in March?"*

Mr. Slade pointed his finger at John. "The President thinks God hates slavery. That's why he wrote them important words. You know, the 'Freedom Bill.'"

John's mustache wriggled. "Oh, yes. Everybody up my way was talking about it. The paper that freed the slaves." He pronounced the words slowly. "E-man-ci-pa-tion Pro-cla-ma-tion. I saw a handbill tacked on a pole."

William laughed. "Glad you can say them words."

The sound of the crowd singing a hymn floated over the field. William reached into his pocket and yanked out a program. "Everett's done talking. After this here

* See the Appendix to read Lincoln's Proclamation.

music, the President has Dedicatory Remarks. I want to hear 'em."

William stuffed his hat back on his head and began taking long strides back toward the platform. John puffed along beside him. Kit Cat's invisible group followed.

William and John slipped into a spot near the platform. Both men took off their hats. Kit Cat's group stayed near the edge of the crowd.

Lincoln, dressed in black, rose to speak. His long face was heavily lined. His somber eyes looked deep into the audience. He glanced down at the sheets of paper he held in his hand. His high tenor voice floated over the crowd. "Four score and seven years ago," he began, "our fathers brought forth on this continent, a new nation, conceived in Liberty, and dedicated to the proposition that all men are created equal..."

One-by-one, the fifth graders dropped to the grass, fascinated by Lincoln's famous Gettysburg Address. Miss Baker didn't move a muscle.

The President's speech barely took three minutes. His voice became stronger as he finished,

"...we here highly resolve that THESE DEAD shall not have died in vain—that this nation, under God, shall have a new birth of freedom—and that government of the people, by the people, for the people, shall not perish from the earth."[1]

He folded his papers and left the podium.

A choir began to sing a dirge—a slow, mournful song for the dead. The beat sounded like the doomed tromp of a funeral march. Then Reverend Baugher closed in prayer.

Before the crowd had a chance to break up, the group from Valley Elementary School slipped away.

"How many people died in the Civil War?" Ben asked as he followed right behind Kit Cat.

"620,000," Mr. Kit Cat said. "The war went on for more than a year after the Battle of Gettysburg."

"For real?" Ben exclaimed, horrified.

"More casualties than all our other wars combined. The Civil War was one of the darkest times in our history."

Sammy's eyes narrowed. "But Lincoln did the right thing, didn't he?"

"Yes, he did," Miss Baker said.

The group took a little rutted road that meandered over the hills. "I heard a great story about Mr. Lincoln," Kit Cat said. "After he was re-elected for a second term as President, there was a reception for him at the White

House. Frederick Douglass came to the door. Frederick had been a slave until age 21. He recruited black troops for the Union army. These soldiers helped the North win the war.

"Frederick had a head of pure-white hair and a strong, clear-eyed face. He was a licensed minister.

"The policemen at the door wouldn't let him in because he was black. When President Lincoln heard that Mr. Douglass was there, he welcomed the minister to the reception. Abraham Lincoln liked Mr. Douglass because both of them had been born poor and fought their way up the ladder of society."

"Did Mr. Douglass like President Lincoln?" Sammy asked.

"Yes, very much. Mr. Douglass didn't agree with everything Mr. Lincoln did, but he admired him greatly."

Miss Baker stopped and faced the group. "Many consider President Lincoln our most religious President," she said. "He prayed for our country. He really believed God would lead and guide us." Her chin tilted up. "I admire him more than any other American."

Silence fell over the group. The breeze rustled the grasses as everyone quietly watched the crowd below leaving the scene.

After a few moments, Kit Cat twitched his tail.

"Whoo hoo!" Marvin shouted as he saw the scene begin to fade. "Here we go again!"

6
One Special Day

The Kit Cat watches suddenly stopped spinning forward. The fifth graders found themselves in a small, square room with large windows on each wall. For a full minute, everyone seemed too stunned to move. Then Marvin ran to the closest window and peered out. "Wow! We're way up high."

The rest joined him and looked out at the sky that seemed close enough to touch and down at the buildings and parks far below.

Elizabeth stepped backward. "I'm afraid of heights," she gasped. Her face was as pale as her blond hair. Laura ran to her side.

"We won't be here for long," Kit Cat soothed. "Look at this while I show the others what we're looking at." He handed the girls a beautifully colored map.

Elizabeth took it gratefully.

Kit Cat padded to the window. "Does anyone know where we are?"

When none of the students answered, Miss Baker said, "This is our nation's capital, Washington, D.C. I believe we're in the Washington Monument."

Kit Cat's arm swept wide to indicate the panoramic scene spread beneath them. "This is the best view in the city."

"I feel like we're in an airplane," Sammy blurted. "The people down there look like ants."

Mary pointed past a ribbon of brownish-green lawn that flowed away from the monument to a huge, white building with a large dome rising from the middle. "What's that building?"

Everyone's eyes followed the direction of her finger.

"The U.S. Capitol," Kit Cat said. "That's where all our laws are made. The House of Representatives meet on one side of the dome and the U.S. Senate meets on the other."

Laura located it on the map.

The students wandered from one window to the next. The second window looked out at a large lake. A small, white building perched on the far end of the lake's edge. "That's the Jefferson Monument," Kit Cat explained.

At the third window, a ribbon of blue water led to another white monument in the distance. It had large, solid columns across its square face. Kit Cat said, "That's the Lincoln Monument."

Scott pushed his nose to the glass. "He sure deserved a monument."

The fifth graders moved to the last window. The park below led to another white building. "And that is the White House," Kit Cat said. "The President of the United States lives and works there."

"The White House," Mary sighed.

Miss Baker shielded her eyes and peered hard through the glass as if she could see through the White House walls. "Believe it or not, the rooms in the White House are named after different colors. There's a blue room and a gold room."

"We may see some of those rooms," Kit Cat hinted. "But now we need to get moving. Let me see your watches."

The students raised their arms high.

"Hang on because we're going to make flying leaps. Pay close attention. This is the most important part of our trip."

The small room exploded into a bright light like a flash bulb going off. Suddenly they were standing in front of a massive, stone building. Large slabs of white stone rose up to the dome on top.

"We're at the Capitol!" Sammy exclaimed.

Tony pointed in the opposite direction to the Washington Monument. "And there's where we were."

The same ribbon of brownish-green park led to a thin, tall white pillar in the distance.

The color drained from Elizabeth's face again. "We really were high up."

Kit Cat patted her on the back. "We won't be going back. C'mon."

The group followed Kit Cat up and down steps around the Capitol. They walked by the crooked limbs of towering trees without leaves and manicured lawns frozen in time by a light frost. As they turned the last corner, the peaceful air was interrupted by bustling activity. The students threaded through a crowd as they climbed the steps leading to the entrance to the Capitol.

"What's going on?" Julie asked as she was almost run over by a huge man tromping down the steps.

Kit Cat stopped near a large white column not far from the entrance. "Today is February 3, 1952. Billy Graham, a great spiritual leader, just finished speaking."

Two men walked up and almost stepped on Miss Baker's invisible shoes. She put her hands up in mock irritation. "Hey guys, watch where you're going."

Kit Cat pointed to the man on the left. "That's Representative Percy Priest."

"Billy Graham can really move an audience," Representative Priest said to his more elderly companion. "I liked his idea to proclaim a day of prayer each year."[1]

"Wouldn't be the first one," his friend said. "Our country has quite a tradition of presidents calling our nation to pray."

Representative Priest thought for a moment. "If our past leaders saw the need to pray, we should too. Tomorrow, I'm going to introduce a resolution calling the President to proclaim a day of prayer."

"Great. I'll support you all the way."

The two men walked into the Capitol. Before they disappeared, the Kit Cat watches flew forward again. Suddenly, everyone found themselves on a brightly lit balcony.

The students cautiously crept up to the railing and peered down at the expansive room below. Four-hundred-thirty-five dark, wooden chairs were precisely lined in rows following the half-moon curve of the huge room. Men with slicked back hair or receding hairlines mingled in clusters or strolled across the room.

Kit Cat pointed to a central area with several desks and a podium placed high on a stage. A huge American flag hung prominently behind it. "We're in the meeting room of the House of Representatives.

This is one of two elected groups who make our national laws. The Speaker of the House sits up there. He makes sure the meeting follows certain rules."

A door to the left of the Speaker's desk opened. Representative Priest entered the room and headed toward his chair.

Marvin spotted a handsome, younger looking man. "There's President Kennedy."

"He's not President yet," Kit Cat said. "Remember, it's 1952. He's still a Representative from the state of Massachusetts."

Miss Baker nodded. "That's right."

Kit Cat faced the group. "Actually, it's February 27, 1952. Two weeks ago, Representative Priest called for a resolution to set aside a day of prayer. Representative Joseph Bryson introduced the resolution. I wanted you to see the proceedings."

Before Kit Cat could say more, a pounding gavel called the meeting to order. The chaplain offered a prayer. As the minutes of the meeting from the day before were read, a few more Congressmen quietly entered the room and slipped into their chairs.

"This is the most important part," Kit Cat whispered as Representative Bryson rose to address the House of Representatives.

"Mr. Speaker," Representative Bryson said, "I ask unanimous consent for the immediate consideration of House Joint Resolution 382 to provide for setting aside an appropriate day as a National Day of Prayer."[2]

The Speaker of the House's voice bellowed from his high position. "Is there objection to the request of the gentleman from South Carolina?"

"I hope no one objects," Oknah whispered.

The students held their breath as one man rose. "Mr. Speaker, reserving the right to object, may I ask the gentleman whether this is a unanimous report from the committee?"

"It is, sir," Representative Bryson said.

The man took his seat. "I withdraw my reservation of the gentleman from South Carolina."

"Thank goodness," Oknah sighed.

The room quieted. Then the Clerk read the joint resolution.

"The President shall set aside and proclaim a suitable day each year, other than a Sunday, as a National Day of Prayer, on which the people of the United States may turn to God in prayer and meditation at churches, in groups, and as individuals."

The joint resolution was read two more times. Then it passed with a loud "Yea" that echoed throughout the large chamber.

Sammy's fist punched the air. "That's it. It's final, right? The National Day of Prayer is law."

Kit Cat shook his head. "Not yet. We have another stop to make."

The watch hands spun again. Everyone felt that elevator-drop sensation in their stomachs.

"Now we're at the other side of the Capitol. In the U.S. Senate," Kit Cat informed them.

The students peered over a similar balcony. Instead of 435 chairs below, they saw one hundred dark, wooden desks.

Seeing her students' confusion, Miss Baker explained, "In the U.S. Senate, there are two Senators from each state. The resolution that passed in the House of Representatives must also pass here."

"Right," Kit Cat said. "It passed here in the Senate on April 17, 1952. Then it was signed by President Truman." He pulled a sheet of paper out of his mysterious pocket. "Here's a copy of the U.S. Senate report* about the resolution." He handed it to Laura.

"Thank you!" She folded it and carefully placed it between the pages of her notebook.

Miss Baker's eyebrows shot up. "There's Lyndon B. Johnson, another future president."

"See the man to his left?" Kit Cat asked.

"I don't believe it. There's Richard Nixon, too."

Kit Cat broke into his half-moon grin. "Yep! Both men supported the National Day of Prayer resolution and then later had the privilege of proclaiming it. You want to see one more President?"

Everyone braced themselves because they knew what was coming next. The watches began whirling, and the large room dissolved into a small garden bordered by green trees and bushes. The afternoon air was thick with the perfume of flowers. Two men were strolling by. One held a stack of papers.

Miss Baker gasped, "President Truman."

"And his aide," Kit Cat said.

The aide pulled out a sheet of paper. "Mr. President, I need your decision on this. Congress passed a resolution

---

* To read the Senate Report, see the Appendix.

calling upon you to set aside one day as a National Day of Prayer. What day would you like?"

President Truman adjusted his glasses and paused to think. Then he smiled. "The Fourth of July." He squinted into the sun which streamed over his aide's shoulder. "The anniversary of the Declaration of Independence. Since the holiday declares our nation's 'firm reliance on the protection of Divine Providence,' I think July Fourth would be perfect. That will be one special day."[4]

"Excellent idea, sir. We'll begin drafting a written proclamation. Can I send out a press release?"

The President nodded. "Please do."

As the aide continued down his list of questions, Kit Cat motioned everyone into a huddle. "The first day chosen was July Fourth. The National Day of Prayer was observed on the Fourth in 1953, too. But the Fourth of July fell on a Sunday in 1954.[5] Why was that a problem?"

Jose's hand shot up like it always did when he knew the answer. "The law said that the President could set aside any day but Sunday."

Kit Cat smiled. "You guys are pretty smart."

"Sure," Marvin said as he strutted with his thumbs under his arms. "We got class."

His words jogged Miss Baker's memory. "Speaking of class, we have a spelling test waiting for us."

The students moaned. Marvin pleaded, "Can't we stay a little longer? I want to see all the monuments."

Miss Baker turned to Kit Cat with a look of despair in her dark eyes. "I think I lost control somehow."

Kit Cat bowed. "I yield to *our* Speaker of the House." The hands on the watches spun forward. The spring garden dissolved, and the fragrant smells drifted away.

The green foliage melted into the familiar chalkboard. The students appeared at their desks, Miss Baker near the board. The Kit Cat Klock ticked normally on the wall.

Everyone seemed frozen in place as if they didn't want to break the spell of what they had just seen.

Miss Baker was the first to recover. She took out her spelling book. "Okay, class, number your papers from one to thirty."

The students reluctantly took out clean sheets of paper. Marvin muttered to himself as he took out his. Before Miss Baker could give the first word, he peered hard at the Kit Cat Klock. "I know you'll be back," he said out loud.

7
The Oval Office and the Gold Room

As she walked into her classroom the next day, Miss Baker almost spilled the pile of graded papers in her arms. During the night, someone had hung a huge photograph on the wall facing the door. The life-sized figures in the picture had startled her.*

Miss Baker set her things on her desk, then crossed the room to study the picture.

* To see this picture, turn to page 153.

Scott and Elizabeth pushed through the door, arguing with each other. Scott stopped dead in his tracks. "Wow, that looks real!" He threw his books on the nearest desk and joined Miss Baker. Elizabeth circled the picture.

"It does look real," Miss Baker replied. Her brown hair brushed her shoulders as she leaned over to look at the picture more closely.

Within minutes, the rest of the class had arrived and were gathered around the photograph. Miss Baker pointed out former President Ronald Reagan. "He must be at his desk in the Oval Office."

"Where's that?" Ben asked.

"It's in the White House."

"We visited the White House," Elizabeth said, "but I don't remember that room."

Miss Baker smiled. "I don't think many people get to see it. Remember the garden where we saw President Truman? That's right next to this office."

Laura followed the line of the beautifully carved desk with her finger. She stopped towards the bottom. "There's Kit Cat's tail," she announced. "What's he doing in the picture?"

All eyes focused on the spot where her finger rested. The tail disappeared, then Kit Cat's head popped out from behind the desk. "I wondered when you'd find me," he beamed. He hopped out of the photograph to a soft landing on his padded paws.

"How did you do that?" Marvin demanded.

"How do I do anything?" Kit Cat answered. His low voice bubbled in his throat and ended in a purr. "Would you like to join me?"

The students shouted, "Yeah!"

Miss Baker got that sly grin on her face. "How can I resist?"

"Got your watches on?" Kit Cat asked. They all raised their arms to show him. He put one foot into the photograph and motioned the class to follow. The watches began to whirl backwards, and the classroom dissolved behind them.

The students found themselves in the middle of a crowded press gallery. At least twenty-five men and women with cameras, tape recorders and note pads surrounded them. Everyone was preparing for the ceremony about to begin at the President's desk.

George pointed to the group around the desk. "Who's with the President?"

"This is the 1988 National Day of Prayer," Kit Cat explained. "Remember when we saw the National Day of Prayer become law in 1952? This year the law is being changed to give the day of prayer a permanent date every year—the first Thursday of every May. President Reagan is about to sign the bill."

"In the middle are Vonette Bright and Pat Boone, the co-chairmen of the National Day of Prayer Task Force which helps inform the nation about the National Day of Prayer. Mrs. Bright is the co-founder of an international missons organization, and Pat Boone is a television personality and singer."

"Who are the other people?" Mary asked.

"The men on the left are U.S. Congressmen who helped get the bill through the House of Representatives that the President is going to sign. The ones on the right are Catholic and Jewish representatives for the National Day of Prayer."

Julie pointed to the middle of the group. "Who's next to Pat Boone? She looks younger than the others."

"That's Susan," Kit Cat replied. "She's the National Coordinator for the day of prayer." He lifted his eyebrow whiskers. "You'd be good at a job like that some day."

Julie's elegant, dark face glowed.

Suddenly the bustling activity in the press gallery stopped.

Mrs. Bright addressed the President and the people in the room. Her eyes sparkled. "As you know, days of prayer have quite a tradition. Since 1952, every president has designated one day each year for prayer. Yet no one knows what that date will be from year to year. President Eisenhower inspired the idea of a regular calendar date for the National Day of Prayer so we could build up a tradition of praying for our country."[1]

Laura furiously scribbled on her note pad.

Pat Boone added, "Mr. President, when the National

Day of Prayer has its own date, every citizen will know when to observe it each year."

President Reagan nodded seriously. "I believe in prayer and feel strengthened by the knowledge that others are asking God's help in my behalf. I can relate to President Lincoln when he said, 'I couldn't for one day face the problems of this office unless I could turn for help to one who is stronger and wiser than all others.'"[2] He picked up his pen.

Kit Cat whispered, "Look! He's about to sign the bill."

"It is my privilege and honor to sign this bill into law," the President announced. He signed the bill using several pens which he handed to those around him. Cameras flashed.

After he finished, the President turned to talk to members of the group around him. Kit Cat led the class out of the Oval Office into a long corridor that had uniformed guards stationed every so many feet.

"Here we go again," Kit Cat said as he flicked his tail. The watches began whirling. Everyone felt the elevator-drop feeling, but nothing seemed changed.

Slipping down the corridor unnoticed by the guards, Kit Cat opened a large door revealing a magnificent golden dining room. "Ladies and gentlemen," Kit Cat presented with a bow, "the Gold Room of the White House."

The Gold Room was so bright compared to the corridor that the students felt like they had walked into streaming sunlight. Everyone blinked to adjust to the brightness.

Kit Cat quickly ushered his group near a wall out of the way of waiters racing by with platters of food and glistening pots brimming with coffee. Breakfast smells drifted in the sunshine coming through the windows.

"The signing of the bill happened in 1988," Kit Cat explained. "Now we're peeking in on the 1989 National Day of Prayer breakfast."

"President and Mrs. Bush!" Miss Baker whispered as she spotted them entering the room.

Kit Cat nodded. "President and Mrs. Bush are honorary chairpersons for the Task Force. They're hosting this National Day of Prayer breakfast." He looked around at the gathering crowd. "There's at least 60 guests."

A tray loaded with food passed close by. Sammy grabbed for a basket of Danish rolls. His hand came up empty.

Tony snickered. "Think an invisible person can eat?"

Sammy shot him a lopsided grin.

Elizabeth and Laura moved near one of the tables. In the center was an elegant arrangement of yellow-and-white flowers that accented the brilliant room. Elizabeth pointed at the china and the nameplates. "Everything's perfect," she whispered.

Gradually, the voices in the room quieted. The students slipped back against the wall.

President Bush went to the podium. "Our obser-vance of a National Day of Prayer reminds us that we can always place our trust in the steady, unfailing light that is the love of God. Our ancestors trusted in the faithfulness of the Almighty, and they frequently turned to Him in humble, heartfelt prayer. When they finally reached these shores, the early settlers gave thanks for their very lives—and for the promise of freedom in a new land."

The President paused. Marvin whispered to George, "The first Thanksgiving. We sure know about that!"

The President continued, "Although much has tran-spired since our ancestors prayed for divine mercy and direction, this occasion calls us to remember, as did Ben Franklin and his contemporaries, that God governs in the affairs of men."

George whispered back to Marvin. "I really thought those men would give up writing the Constitution. How about you?"

Marvin nodded.

"The One to whom George Washington turned when he knelt in the snow at Valley Forge," the President emphasized, "is the same God who heard the prayers of President Lincoln nearly a century later during the darkest hours of the Civil War."

Marvin and George gave each other knowing looks.

"While our needs today may be different, we are no less dependent on the help of Almighty God. Therefore, let us likewise seek His forgiveness, strength, and guid-ance."[3]

The guests bowed their heads as prayers were offered for the nation.

After a moment of silence, the guests began mingling. Kit Cat and his group stepped back into the corridor.

"Is this the only event on the National Day of Prayer?" Ben asked.

"Oh, no!" Kit Cat assured him. "People celebrate this day all across the nation in all kinds of ways." He glanced at his watch. "The National Day of Prayer is only a week away. Why don't we go to a few events?"

Miss Baker put her arm around Kit Cat's shoulder. "And what about the Math test a week from Friday? We haven't gone over the material."

Marvin pleaded, "We promise we'll study hard."

Scott added, "Sounds like fun."

Kit Cat smiled. "I have a special kind of transportation to get us around."

"What is it?" Mary asked.

Kit Cat just shook his head. "Can't tell," he said. "But it'll be quite an experience."

Miss Baker looked at her excited students. "How can I say no?"

Everyone cheered.

Kit Cat curved his tail and the watches began whirling. The wallpaper in the corridor became a stream of rainbow colors as the scene began to fade.

8

Breakfast at the Grand Hotel

While the fifth grade class was in the White House, trouble was brewing in their classroom. Principal McDonald checked on the rooms in his school building every day. He did this at different times, depending on his schedule. Today his ten o'clock appointment canceled so he left the office early.

He strode down the hall with long steps. His navy blue suit hung neatly from his shoulders, and his thin brown hair was combed smoothly over his bald spot. He carefully peered into each classroom door window so he wouldn't disturb the class.

When he reached Miss Baker's room, he glanced through the window. The room was empty.

Mr. McDonald stuck his head in the room. Not a student anywhere. The only sound was the plain black clock ticking loudly on the wall.

Mr. McDonald rubbed his chin. His high forehead wrinkled into deep frown lines. "Where on earth did everyone go?" he wondered aloud. "I know Miss Baker didn't sign out for a field trip."

He walked around Miss Baker's desk, looking for some clue to where the class might have gone. The only thing he saw was the huge picture on the chalkboard.

"I'd better find out what happened," he said as he rushed out the door. Just as he shut it, he heard a noise. Peeking back in through the small window, he saw the students and Miss Baker sitting calmly at their desks.

For a moment, Mr. McDonald didn't move. Then he rubbed his eyes and looked again. He cracked open the door and stuck in his nose. "Miss Baker?" he asked

Miss Baker crinkled her nose. "Yes?"

Mr. McDonald sauntered over to Miss Baker's desk. "Everything fine here?"

One-by-one, the students slipped their math books out of their desks and buried their noses deep in the pages.

Miss Baker smiled weakly. "Yes. We're just starting our math lesson."

"So I see." Rubbing his hand over his chin, he turned

to go. Just before he opened the door, he looked around and said, "Carry on." Then he left.

When the door clicked shut, sighs of relief rose all over the room. It looked as if Mr. McDonald had put the strange things he had seen out of his mind.

For the next few days, Miss Baker's classroom buzzed about the Pilgrims, the Continental Congress, and the visit to Washington, D.C. Everyone asked to see Laura's notes. But no one dared mention the close call with Mr. McDonald.

The National Day of Prayer dawned bright and sunny. The students arrived in their classroom early.

Just before the bell rang, Mr. McDonald pulled an adult-sized desk into the room. He spread some papers over the top, sat in the desk and began to work.

"What's he doing?" Marvin whispered to Sammy.

"I don't know. Think he's checking us out?"

Marvin shrugged. "Maybe."

When the bell rang, Miss Baker took attendance. The students kept taking quick glances at Mr. McDonald.

After they recited the *Pledge of Allegiance,* Miss Baker announced, "Our principal will be joining our class this morning. He spends one day every school year in each room. We are privileged to have him with us today."

Faces all over the room dropped like balloons emptied of helium. Mary leaned over to Laura. "No Kit Cat today," she whispered.

Laura could barely keep the tears from her eyes.

As the day's math lesson went on, Mr. McDonald continued working on his papers. He peered around the room every few minutes, noticing everything.

Miss Baker wrote some math problems on the blackboard. Mr. McDonald's eyes drifted to the Kit Cat Klock.

The Klock winked.

Mr. McDonald's eyes bugged out.

Soft giggling snaked through the rows of students.

Mr. McDonald ignored the Klock for several moments, then glanced at it again. It winked at him a second time. Mr. McDonald gasped and dropped his pencil. Miss

Baker stopped writing in the middle of a division problem and turned to see what the commotion was about.

Suddenly, Kit Cat hopped down from the Klock. He casually sat on the principal's desk top and crossed his legs. Mr. McDonald just stared, his face frozen.

Kit Cat beamed his wide grin and explained to the principal how the class had been learning about the history of prayer in the United States. "We've been taking time-travel trips to many places. You can join us if you put on this special watch." Kit Cat held out a Kit Cat watch.

The principal stared at it. He wouldn't take the watch. Turning to Miss Baker, he asked, "Is this for real?"

"You bet your life it is," she replied.

The entire room seemed paralyzed for a moment. No one knew how to handle the situation. Even Kit Cat was quiet. Then Mr. McDonald's mouth split into a grin. "So that's where you were the other day." He fumbled with the watchband until he had it fastened snugly around his wrist. "I can't believe I'm doing this," he exclaimed. "This is crazy!"

"Come see what I've got outside!" Kit Cat said as he hopped off the desk and headed to the door.

Everybody followed him. When they reached the sidewalk near the school loading zone, Kit Cat said, "Wait here!" and disappeared behind the building.

Everyone buzzed with curiosity.

"What do you think Kit Cat went to get?" Elizabeth asked.

"It'll be a spaceship," Tony declared, his wavy brown hair blowing in the breeze whipping around the corner of the school building.

"No, I think it'll be a solar-powered limo or a huge skateboard with rocket engines attached," Marvin added.

Mr. McDonald muttered as he paced the sidewalk, hands deep in his pants pockets. His thin, graying hair stayed perfectly in place in the breeze.

Miss Baker was the first to spot Kit Cat. "There he is!" she exclaimed. "In the yellow school bus."

"Not a school bus," Scott moaned.

Outside, the bus did look pretty ordinary. But as they filed up the stairs, the children saw a dashboard filled with lighted buttons and flashing dials. "Time control panel," Kit Cat explained from the captain's chair.

The inside of the bus looked like a cat's paradise. The floor was soft and woody, easy on padded paws. The seats were upholstered with all kinds of fake fur: tabby, Siamese, striped, calico, even Persian.

"Cool!" Jose exclaimed as he headed for a jet-black seat.

The students, Miss Baker and Mr. McDonald strapped themselves into furry comfort. Kit Cat's tail lightly tapped the floor as he punched buttons, flipped levers and rotated dials like an expert fighter pilot. Sammy, who had picked the seat right behind Kit Cat, leaned over to watch.

The bus began rumbling as if something was roiling and boiling deep in its engine. The windows misted.

Mary peered out as the school turned into blur of color. She bounced in her seat as the bus lurched and shuddered. Within seconds, Kit Cat brought the bus to an abrupt stop. Everyone jerked forward in their seats.

Climbing out, Kit Cat stood in front of the elegant entrance to a high-rise building. "Welcome to the Grand Hotel and the Mayor's Prayer Breakfast." They all followed Kit Cat across the lobby and into a huge ballroom.

Inside, the noise of greetings buzzed everywhere. More than 800 people were milling around tables. Banners of red, white and blue were draped like streamers across the high ceiling. Huge chandeliers glistened like giant prisms, reflecting the patriotic colors in the room.

Kit Cat led the group through the maze of guests to a table at the front of the room near the stage. He picked up a crisp white brochure with blue printing neatly resting on the red linen tablecloth. "Here's the program and a copy of the President's words about the National Day of Prayer. On the right, you'll see the schedule for the breakfast."

Sammy's big brown eyes widened as he noticed the menu. "Unreal! There's so much food!"

Running her eyes down the long schedule, Mary sighed, "We'll be here all morning."

Kit Cat looked down at Mary. "I promise it will be a very interesting morning." He picked up a small card laying beside a plate. "This is a bookmark you can keep. On one side, it lists specific things you can pray for our nation, and on the other, some encouragement to pray."[1]

Mary turned her bookmark over and read a verse from the Bible printed on it: "If My people who are called by My name will humble themselves and pray, and seek My face and turn from their wicked ways, then I will hear from heaven, will forgive their sin, and will heal their land (2 Chronicles 7:14)." She stuck it in her pocket.

As the students selected their seats, Kit Cat said, "I must warn you that everyone can see you now. I'm the only invisible one." Then he slipped away outside.

A distinguished-looking man walked up to the table. "Mayor Green. It's good to see you!" Mr. McDonald exclaimed.

The two men shook hands warmly. Turning to the class, the principal said, "I'd like you to meet my fifth grade class and their teacher, Miss Baker."

"I already know this one," Mayor Green said as he gave Julie a bear hug. "I don't know what I'd do without your father. He performs miracles as my Scheduling Assistant. Does he know you're here?"

"Actually, he doesn't," Julie said. "I didn't know I'd be here."

The mayor's friendly eyes continued around the table as Mr. McDonald introduced everyone. Noticing Oknah's oriental features and her accent, Mayor Green asked, "Are you from Korea by any chance?"

"Yes," she replied shyly.

"How long have you lived in the United States?"

"Two years."

"Do you know about Prayer Mountain?"

Oknah nodded, obviously pleased.

"Have you ever visited one?"

"Yes, once before we moved to America. I was only nine."

George shoved his glasses higher on his nose. "People in Korea go to mountains to pray?" he quizzed Oknah.

"Yes," she said. "People there pray a lot. They go to what we call Prayer Mountain. There they enjoy the beauty of God's creation. They pray in peace and silence for hours or days."

"It's a beautiful idea," Mayor Green said sincerely. "I have a 'prayer chair' in my office at home where I go every morning to pray. It's winged-back with high sides. When I sit in it, I feel very secluded. Just me and God."

He glanced at the head table on stage. "It looks like the breakfast is ready to start. It was nice talking with you." He smiled at Julie as he turned to leave. "I'll be sure to tell your father you're here."

Oknah leaned toward George. "I'm going to tell my parents about the mayor's prayer chair."

A voice boomed over the loud speaker, "Take your seats, please." After the blessing, the students nibbled at the eggs, ham and rolls set before them. While they ate, the emcee introduced the mayor.

Mayor Green's voice sounded crisp and sure. "Welcome to the 35th Annual Prayer Breakfast," he announced proudly. "Our city is a checkerboard of many different people. Today's observance of the National Day of Prayer has great promise to help make us 'one' as a country. I am personally grateful that our oneness is centered around a most important freedom in our United States of America—the freedom to pray."[2]

The class listened carefully as the Mayor and other civic and religious leaders spoke. The choirs sang and men and women prayed for the nation, its leaders, its people, and its needs.

Soon the last speaker on the agenda was announced: Retired Admiral George Lewis, former prisoner of war. He looked dignified in his crisp uniform. His medals of honor twinkled in the lights streaming over the stage.

"I was a fighter pilot on an aircraft carrier during the Vietnam War," he began. "I was shot down during my second combat tour over North Vietnam. As my parachute slowly drifted down into enemy territory, I didn't know if I would live or die!" His handsome face saddened. "I had heard so many horrible stories about the North Vietnamese prison camps. At that moment, I was so glad God was with me."

He smiled faintly. "Fortunately, I wasn't killed, but little did I know what I would endure during the next eight years." His voice trembled. "I was tortured fifteen times, held in leg irons for two years, and kept in solitary confinement for four years. But that wasn't the worst part of my sufferings. It was the loneliness of not seeing my family and friends."

He paused for a moment, obviously trying to collect himself, then went on. "Sometimes I sat in my dark, cold cell and wondered about my wife. How was she managing? Did she still miss me? On my daughter's birthdays, I'd picture her with a cake, laughing and giggling with all her friends. As the years went by, I tried to imagine what she looked like as a ten-year-old, eleven- or twelve-year-old, and as a teenager. I thought about my son. My heart ached because I couldn't throw a baseball with him or take him on a fishing trip.

"God became my closest friend. When it seemed I couldn't do anything for my family, I realized I could do the greatest thing for them—pray. I spent days praying for my family.

"I also prayed for my country. Without newspapers or television, I was totally out of touch. Who was president? Were we still involved in the war? Did anyone in government know I was here?

"No matter how brutal conditions became, no one could make me quit praying. Or chase God out of my cell. Prayer was my one link to my family, friends and country. And I knew they were praying for me."

He smiled. "Of course, I also prayed to be found. How grateful I am that God hears and answers prayer. And for the freedom to pray."[3]

Admiral Lewis closed with a moving prayer. After he finished, the guests began slowly leaving, their conversation hushed.

Oknah had tears in her eyes as she got up from her seat. "My parents don't have to have a Prayer Mountain to pray either. They brought their prayers with them to America."

Mr. McDonald smiled at her. "You bet."

Suddenly, Kit Cat reappeared as quietly as he had gone. He was wearing a distinguished-looking top hat.

Marvin raced up to him. "Can you believe that guy? A fighter pilot shot down. Eight years in prison. Tortured fifteen times." Marvin shook his head in amazement. "I'd go crazy."

George added thoughtfully, "It's true. No matter what, God is always there to listen."

Julie's father approached. She had obviously gotten her dark, finely-etched features and tall, elegant poise from him.

"Kit Cat," Mary said, alarmed. "Hide!"

Kit Cat laughed. "He can't see me."

Sure enough, Mr. Jackson didn't notice Kit Cat. He gently kissed Julie on the forehead and took her slender hands in his. "Honey, when Admiral Lewis was talking, I was thinking about what it would be like if I didn't see you for eight years. I don't tell you enough how special you are to me."

Julie hugged him. "I love you too, Daddy." Then she ran to catch up with her classmates heading for the bus.

9

Rally at Noon

"Where are we off to next?" Jose asked excitedly as he reached for the railing on the bus stairway. The bright morning sun bounced off the windows of the Grand Hotel behind him.

Sammy poked Jose to hurry him along. "We'd know sooner if you get moving."

Jose ran up the few steps followed by the other fifth graders. Miss Baker and Mr. McDonald were the last to get on. Kit Cat grinned from his captain's chair as they threaded their way to the seats. Then he stepped into the aisle. "Our next stop is the state capital to join a noon prayer rally on the Capitol steps!"

Oknah exclaimed, "I've never been there before!"

"I have," Elizabeth responded confidently. "It's neat. My uncle's a state senator. He took me and my family on a tour of the Capitol building last year." Her eyes lit up. "I could call him. I bet he'd show us around."

"Sounds good," Kit Cat said. He motioned her to the front of the bus where a cellular phone rested on the dashboard.

Elizabeth dialed her uncle's office. After a pause, she said, "Uncle Mike. This is Elizabeth." After explaining her plan, she hung up and announced, "He'll meet us at the Capitol steps just before the rally."

Kit Cat took the driver's seat. "We have a little time. Let's drive to the capital the regular way." He started the engine and pulled away from the hotel.

In an hour, the bus turned onto the long drive leading to the front of the Capitol building. The students saw manicured lawns, sculptured bushes and a massive white stone building ahead of them.

Kit Cat stopped and let everyone off the bus. Then he got off himself. Looking at his watch, he exclaimed, "No time to find a parking lot." He tapped the face of his Kit Cat watch, and the bus disappeared.

Marvin, who had been leaning against the fender, cried, "Whoa" as he almost fell off the curb. He turned to stare at the empty parking spot.

George tapped the face of his Kit Cat watch to see if he could make something disappear.

Kit Cat smiled slyly. "Good thing your watch doesn't do everything mine does. You'd have made the whole Capitol disappear."

Tony smirked. "I wish I had Kit Cat's watch. I could make my sister disappear. Or my report card!"

George and Jose laughed.

Elizabeth spotted her uncle and ran to greet him. State Senator Mike Miller was a tall, handsome man with blond hair like Elizabeth's. She took his hand and led him to the class. "This is our teacher Miss Baker, our principal Mr. McDonald, and my fifth grade class."

He shook Miss Baker's and Mr. McDonald's hands. "So nice to meet you. Let me show you around before the rally starts. We'll use the side entrance. Everyone's pretty busy setting up on the front steps."

Sure enough, scurrying workmen were busy hanging up banners and putting finishing touches on a large platform built just outside the main entrance. The Senator led the class down a wide sidewalk to a set of double wooden doors. He held the door open as they filed into a cool hallway.

He directed them to the huge domed center of the capitol building. They lined up around a large circle set in the flooring.

Pointing to the circle, Senator Miller explained, "This is our state seal." Looking up, he continued, "This dome goes up twenty stories. The writing around the rim of the upper dome reads 'In God We Trust' just like the motto on our money."

Elizabeth pulled a dollar bill out of her jacket. Ben found a nickel in his pants pocket.

They compared the same phrase printed on the money.

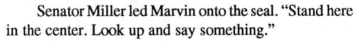

Senator Miller led Marvin onto the seal. "Stand here in the center. Look up and say something."

Marvin spotted Kit Cat leaning against a column. He looked up and said, "Kit Cat."

"Kiiiittt Caaattt," echoed back loud and clear.

Several other students took turns standing on the seal and hearing their voices echo. When they finished, Senator Miller led the class down two long corridors. He described the duties of the different departments in the state government printed on the doors.

Miss Baker turned to Mr. McDonald. "This certainly will cover this week's social studies lesson."

He grinned.

Senator Miller took the class to the front entrance. As the students stepped out of the massive doors, they saw a large crowd assembled on the fifty steps leading up to the entrance. They carefully maneuvered around the brightly decorated platform and down a few steps to a place in front of the crowd.

Wide-eyed, the students surveyed the scene. A huge American flag waved above the doors. Its colors stood out against the sparkling white stone of the building. Several banners hung over the platform with the theme of the rally, "Praying for Our Leaders," written in huge red letters.

To the left, three high school bands in full uniform stood at attention. The combined band started playing patriotic songs. The warm sun mixed with a slightly cool breeze which fluttered the banners.

Julie and Elizabeth surveyed the crowd below them.

"There's a family that came from India," Julie said, pointing to a woman dressed in long flowing fabric with a red dot on her forehead.

Elizabeth spotted some businessmen. "I bet they're from China."

"No, I think they're from Japan," Oknah corrected her.

Soon the three girls were playing a game to see who could spot the most national heritages.

A hush came over the crowd as four elderly men in sharply-ironed uniforms making up a Color Guard marched up the steps through an aisle in the crowd. Near a large column, they turned as one and placed the flag in a stand. Stepping back, they saluted the flag and led the people in the Pledge of Allegiance. Then one of the soldiers placed an elegant flower wreath beneath the flag.

"Those soldiers are war veterans," Senator Miller whispered. "The flowers are in honor of those who died for peace."

Theresa Mendosa, the woman who organized the gathering, was introduced. She greeted the crowd. "Welcome to this observance of the National Day of Prayer. We are continuing a rich history of prayer. Recently, I found a copy of an article from the January 20, 1905, edition of the *Denver Post*. The front page headline reads, 'Entire City Pauses for Prayer Even at the High Tide of Business.'"[1]

She held up the article. "The column says, 'The marts of trade were deserted between noon and two o'clock this afternoon, and all worldly affairs were forgotten, and the entire city was given over to meditation of higher things. Seldom has such a remarkable sight been witnessed—an entire city, in the middle of a busy weekday, bowing before the throne of heaven and asking and receiving the blessing of the King of the Universe.'"

She stretched her arms over the audience. "Here we are, assembled almost one hundred years later. We too have left our work places and our homes to come together to pray for our nation and its leaders.

"But before we pray, our Governor will share the National Day of Prayer State Proclamation."

The crowd applauded as Governor Smith thanked Theresa. He held up an elegantly written document and read the words on it.

When he finished, he looked down at the huge crowd in front of him. "My wife and I have looked for ways to encourage a greater understanding of prayer in our nation's history among our youth. After hearing about the National Day of Prayer essay contest sponsored by KXYZ, we invited the winning classes from across the state to a brunch at the governor's mansion." His face broke into a smile. "We look forward to meeting these students."

Marvin turned to Sammy. "We've just got to win."

Oknah and Julie nodded enthusiastically.

After the Governor finished speaking, Theresa called on several pastors and civic dignitaries to pray for leaders in all levels of government, business and churches in the community. Hundreds of heads bowed as everyone joined in the prayer.

A black gospel choir filed onto the platform. The

choir director raised his hands, and the choir burst into "This Land Is Your Land." Their bodies swayed with the music, and their hands beat with the rhythm.

Someone in the audience began clapping to the music and soon the entire crowd joined in. The choir increased the tempo on a second time through the song, and the audience began singing too. It seemed as if the choir and the crowd had melted into one, singing about the land they loved.

A heavy woman with a shining face stepped out in front of the choir. Her clear, sparkling voice sang "The Star Spangled Banner."

When the last crystal note of the anthem faded, Theresa closed in prayer. Then she announced, "Thank you for using your lunch break to observe the National Day of Prayer. Many of us will visit our state leaders and judges during the next few hours to pray for them specifically. If you'd like to join us, we would be pleased to have you. Thanks again for being here. God bless you!"

The high school bands burst into a patriotic tribute as the crowd began to break up.

Senator Miller led his guests to meet Theresa. After the introductions, Laura pulled out her note pad. "Are there other gatherings like this?"

Theresa's eyes sparkled. "Actually, there are at least twenty-five rallies at other state capitals taking place right now. Many other people who don't live near state capitals are meeting at city halls to pray."

After shuffling through her briefcase, Theresa handed Laura some papers. "Here's a state-by-state list of observances taking place across our nation today."[2]

Laura flipped through the pages. "There sure are a lot of things going on! Thanks. This will help us write our essay for the contest."

Theresa shut her briefcase and smiled. "I had a feeling you were participating in the essay contest. When the Governor mentioned it, you all looked pretty determined."

Marvin broke in. "You bet! We're going to win."

Miss Baker put her arm around Marvin's shoulders. "Would you believe he objected the loudest when I first mentioned the project?"

Everyone laughed, including Marvin.

Mr. McDonald interrupted. "Our bus is waiting for us at the bottom of the steps." He shook Theresa's and Senator Miller's hands. "Thank you for everything. This has been an experience."

Marvin shouted, "Let's race to the bottom," and loped down the first few steps.

The rest of the students bolted after him, threading their way around the groups of people still talking. Miss Baker and Mr. McDonald followed at a normal pace.

"Where are we going next?" he asked her.

"I don't know," Miss Baker answered confidently, "but it's sure to be good."

10

Youth Set City Ablaze

Tony and Marvin flew down the last few steps of the Capitol, neck and neck. Their legs pumped hard like pistons in an engine. Mary and Sammy sped along right behind them.

Tony touched the side of the bus first. Marvin, a close second, leaned against the bus to catch his breath. Mary passed Sammy in the last two feet. She beamed a triumphant smile.

Kit Cat hopped out of the bus and landed softly on the curb beside them. He announced in his sportscaster's voice, "And for the winner, we have a medal." He hung a yellow ribbon around Tony's neck. The medal at the bottom was a quarter glued to yellow construction paper in the shape of a star. The shiny coin glistened in the sunlight.

Kit Cat grinned. "Not bad for such short notice. Be careful. The glue's still wet."

Tony peered at the quarter. "Here it is again. 'In God We Trust.'"

Mary laughed. "What a great way to remember today."

Kit Cat scooped the winner onto his shoulders. Tony flexed his muscles as Kit Cat carried him once around the bus.

Soon the rest of the class had gathered near the bus door.

"Who's hungry?" Kit Cat asked as he gently put Tony back on the pavement.

The students shouted, "I am."

Mr. McDonald looked at his watch. "It's after twelve."

"We're going to have my favorite food today," Kit Cat purred.

Marvin had a look of horror on his face. "I hope it's not fish sandwiches."

Kit Cat grinned from ear to ear. "Actually, I like hamburgers."

Everyone cheered.

"Lunch is on the bus," Kit Cat said as he bounded up the steps.

Each person found a lunch bag on his seat that contained a hamburger, apple, large cookie and a can of soda pop.

"Pull the green string on the seat on front of you, and a little table will flip down," Kit Cat explained.

"Just like an airplane," Julie exclaimed as her little table slid out perfectly in front of her.

"Cool," Sammy said. "I wish our school bus had these."

The fifth grade class dug into their lunches. Kit Cat finished first, wiped his whiskers with his napkin, and spun the captain's chair around to face the class. He held up a newspaper. "See this headline? It says, 'Youth Set City Ablaze.' It's about the National Day of Prayer.

"Some high school students decided to make an impact on their community on the day of prayer. Some are at the hospitals visiting and praying with the patients. Others are at shopping malls with tables of information. There's also a group at a nursing home. I thought we'd stop by and see how they're doing."

Mr. McDonald smiled. "What a terrific idea."

"We're headed across state," Kit Cat said as he whirled around in his chair, "so buckle up and hang onto your drinks."

The bus rumbled. The windows misted and the Capitol building disappeared like a puff of smoke.

Kit Cat stopped the bus abruptly. After he parked it, the students followed him up a trim walkway to a plantation-style porch on a sprawling building where a large poster read, "Pray for Our Nation."

Kit Cat opened the door to let the students by and then settled into a rocker on the porch to wait. The others entered a wide foyer decorated with potted plants.

A gangly high-school-aged boy greeted them. "Hi. I'm Larry."

Larry turned to Miss Baker and Mr. McDonald. "Are you here to help with the National Day of Prayer?"

Both adults nodded.

"We'd like to see what you do," Mr. McDonald suggested.

Larry looked delighted. "Why don't we visit a few of the folks here?" Surveying the class size, he suggested, "I'll take half of you." He pointed to a petite brown-haired girl approaching him from the right hallway. "We'll ask Virginia to show the others around."

They split into two groups. Virginia and Mr. McDonald led their students down the right hallway. Miss Baker and Larry went down the left one. Both groups stopped several times to talk and pray with the residents in the halls.

As Miss Baker's group approached an open door decorated with artistic greeting cards, Larry whispered, "We must stop here. Mrs. Wilson has been a real inspiration to me."

Inside the room, an old woman was sitting in a wheelchair near a window box filled with bright yellow daisies. The deep lines on her face turned into smile wrinkles when she saw the students. Her aged, spotted hands were resting on a red, white and blue afghan which covered her legs and front of her wheelchair. "My, my, who do we have here?" she said in her wavery voice.

Larry introduced Miss Baker and the students. Everyone found a place to sit, either in a chair or on the bed. Laura pulled her chair close to Mrs. Wilson.

Looking around at the many patriotic paintings on the wall, Julie exclaimed, "These are beautiful. Who's the artist?"

Mrs. Wilson blushed. "I did these in my younger days. I've always had a fascination with history. I traveled to Washington, D.C., several times to paint our national monuments."

Ben pointed to a large painting of the Statue of Liberty. The colors in the sky melted together like a soft rainbow. "I like that one best."

Mrs. Wilson nodded. "I like that one, too. See the quote underneath it?"

Ben walked over and looked closely.

"It was written in the 1800's by a French Statesman named Alexis de Tocqueville," Mrs. Wilson said. "Later, France gave the United States the Statue of Liberty to put in the New York harbor. Alexis came to America to find the secret to our greatness. He searched and searched.

Please read the last few lines where he explains where he found it."

Ben followed the fancy letters down with his finger, then read,

"Not until I went into the churches of America and heard her pulpits aflame with righteousness did I understand the secret of her genius and power. America is great because America is good, and if America ever ceases to be good, America will cease to be great."[1]

"That's why I think the National Day of Prayer is so important," Mrs. Wilson added thoughtfully. "It reminds us of our need to seek God's wisdom as a nation."

George walked over to a black-and-white painting of the Lincoln Memorial. "President Lincoln asked for God's help when our country almost split in two because of slavery." He pointed to a painting of the Constitutional Convention. "And Ben Franklin asked the delegates to pray when the convention was breaking up."

Mrs. Wilson turned to Miss Baker. "I'm impressed."

"We have learned a lot," Miss Baker admitted.

Larry knelt beside Mrs. Wilson. "Tell the kids what prayer means to you."

Mrs. Wilson thought for a moment. "Since God made me, He knows me. He knows how I operate and how a nation operates. God loves us so much, He wants us to talk to Him. He answers prayer—not always in the way we ask—but always in the best way."

She rested her wrinkled hand on Laura's hand.

"Since my body is old, I'm not very active any more. But I can have a ministry of prayer. I spend a lot of time looking at my paintings and praying for our country. I pray for our President, his Cabinet members and many other leaders by name. I pray that they will listen to God as they go about their business. I also pray for young people that they would live a life pleasing to God."

She patted Laura's hand. "You are our future leaders."

"But what if we do something wrong?" George asked. "Doesn't God get angry?"

Smile wrinkles fluttered across Mrs. Wilson's face. "I wouldn't call Him angry. But He is hurt. Have you ever done something your mom and dad told you not to do?"

"Once I left my glasses on the floor, and my dad stepped on them," George admitted. "I had to go two days without glasses. My mom wouldn't let me watch TV or videos. Boy! Did I wish I had listened to her!"

"That's an excellent example," Mrs. Wilson said. "Your parents don't give you rules because they're mean, but to protect you. God is like that. He wants the best for us so He gives us guidelines. When we do mess up, all we have to do is tell Him we are truly sorry, and He will forgive us."

Mary looked at Mrs. Wilson. "I've heard a lot of people pray, but if I were by myself, I wouldn't know what to say."

Mrs. Wilson pulled a Bible off the window ledge

and opened it to a marked page. "Talk to God like you would to a good friend. If you're not sure what to say, follow the prayer Jesus taught His disciples to use. It's in Matthew chapter six, verses nine through thirteen." She tapped her fingers on the passage in her Bible.

Mary took the Bible and read the marked place.

"Mrs. Wilson, why don't I pray for you since you're always praying for everyone else?" Larry suggested.

Her eyes lit up.

Larry bowed his head. "Thank you, Lord, for Mrs. Wilson. Protect her and continue to give her good health. Give her strength to continue in this ministry of prayer. We thank you for the National Day of Prayer. Help us to remember to pray for our country, not only today, but throughout the year. Amen."

Mrs. Wilson had tears in her eyes when they looked up again.

Mary walked over and gave her a big hug. "You remind me of my Grandma. She died last year. Could I kind of adopt you like we did my brother?"

"I'd like that," Mrs. Wilson responded, color flooding her cheeks.

Mary's face lit up. "Could we write to each other?"

"I'd love that," Mrs. Wilson said softly.

Mary and Mrs. Wilson exchanged addresses. The students said good-bye and left Mrs. Wilson holding her Bible in her lap. Rays of sunshine streamed through the windows making her white-gray hair glow.

"She looks like an angel," Julie whispered to Mary as they waved one last good-bye before heading for the bus.

"She sure does," Mary said softly as she turned to go.

11
Ten Seconds Till Air Time!

"Look at that silly cat!" Elizabeth exclaimed as she and Julie walked out the front door of the nursing home. "He's sound asleep."

The early afternoon sun shone in wide rays through the porch rails like crepe paper streamers. They fell in a line on the floor. Kit Cat's rocking chair stuck half-way into the sunshine. His toes were toasty warm; his face was in the shade.

105

The other students banged through the door. Their rowdy conversations dwindled to a whisper when they saw Kit Cat snoozing.

"Should we wake him?" Julie asked.

Sammy's mouth slid into a crooked grin. He picked up a long, black crow's feather that had blown up against the wooden railings. "Let's tickle his feet." He stroked the feather up and down the bare bottoms of Kit Cat's furry paws.

Kit Cat smiled slightly like he was having a good dream. Then the smile turned into a soft purr. The purr broke into a chuckle. Soon he was laughing hysterically. He looked so funny that the students started laughing with him.

"What's going on here?" Mr. McDonald asked as he and Miss Baker joined the students on the porch.

Kit Cat sat up straight. "I guess someone was kind enough to wake me from my nap."

The students giggled.

After stretching, Kit Cat looked at his watch. "We'd better get a move on!"

The students raced down the sidewalk to the bus, claiming seats near the windows as they pushed through the door.

After everyone was seated and buckled up, Kit Cat spun around his captain's chair. "Hang on. Now we're going to see how a radio station promotes the National Day of Prayer."

"Is it KXYZ?" Scott shouted, squirming excitedly in his seat.

"Sure is," Kit Cat grinned. "I knew your father managed the station so I made an appointment for us to meet him today."

"He didn't even tell me," Scott said, surprised.

Kit Cat whirled his chair into driving position. "Of course not! Today is kind of a 'mystery ramble.' I know where we're going, but you don't. How do you like it so far?"

The students clapped, whistled and cheered.

Scott turned to Tony. "This will be great. Seeing my dad at work."

Kit Cat began to flip levers and push buttons. The engine rumbled, and the windows misted. The riders were pushed deep into their furry chairs.

Scott squinted through the mist. In seconds, he saw the radio station and its antenna coming up fast. "This is it," he said smugly.

A friendly receptionist greeted Miss Baker, Mr. McDonald and the students as they walked through the front door of the radio station. "How can I help you?" she asked.

Scott walked up to the desk. "We're here to see my dad, Randy Sullivan."

The receptionist pushed her glasses further down on her nose and peered at Scott over them. "So you're Scott.

Your dad talks about you all the time." She picked up her phone and told his father they were in the lobby.

A few minutes later, Mr. Sullivan opened the door. He was as big as a lineman on a pro football team. But his warm smile made him seem as soft as a puffy marshmallow. "Hello, there!" He gave Scott a huge pat on the back. "Glad you all could come."

Scott quickly introduced his dad to everyone. Then Mr. Sullivan led them to a large conference room. They took seats around a shiny, black table.

"What's the station doing to celebrate the National Day of Prayer?" Mr. McDonald asked.

"Several things," Mr. Sullivan said. "We're sponsoring the essay contest you all are working on. We're also sponsoring a poetry contest for younger school children. In fact, the winners will be here at three-thirty to read their poems over the air. We've also been broadcasting the public service announcements the National Day of Prayer Task Force sends us. Would you like to hear one?"

"Sure," Marvin blurted.

Mr. Sullivan opened a cabinet door built into the wall. He pushed a button, and several lights came on a stereo system. The speakers in the four corners of the room began to crackle and pop. Then a voice filled the room.

"Hi! This is Pat Boone. Throughout the history of the United States, men and women have prayed in times of crisis and times of thanksgiving, in need and in plenty.

Prayer has been practiced and recommended without reservation by our people. Join with Americans throughout our nation on the first Thursday of every May in celebrating our fundamental freedom to pray."[1]

Mr. Sullivan turned off the stereo.

"He sounds so real," Sammy gasped. "Just like he's in the room."

"I feel like we're back in the Oval Office listening to him talk to President Reagan," Scott said.

The room fell silent at Scott's blunder. He blushed.

Mr. Sullivan burst into a belly-laugh. "Son, you have quite an imagination."

The others laughed too, relieved that Scott's father hadn't guessed their secret.

Mr. Sullivan frowned. "So tell me, what have you learned about the National Day of Prayer so far?"

Scott did a half-turn in his swivel chair. "We learned about the first Thanksgiving. The Pilgrims thanked God for the bounty of the land."

Elizabeth pushed back a stray piece of her blond hair. "Many of our Founding Fathers turned to God. George Washington prayed during the Revolutionary War, and Abraham Lincoln called several days of prayer during the Civil War."

"Don't forget Ben Franklin," Ben interrupted, "and how he asked the delegates to pray when they were about to give up writing the Constitution."

Laura read from her notes. "In 1952 both houses of Congress called upon the President to set aside one day each year as a National Day of Prayer."

Julie piped up, "But in 1988, a bill passed making it the first Thursday of every May."

"You all know more about the National Day of Prayer than I do," Mr. Sullivan said. "You should share some of this on the air." He glanced at the huge clock on the wall. "How about right now?"

Marvin bounced in his seat. "I've always wanted to be a disc jockey!"

"Why don't you do the interview?" Mr. Sullivan suggested.

Marvin bolted out of his chair. "Wow, I better call my friends and tell them I'll be on the air."

Mr. McDonald put an arm around his shoulder. "They're all in school, Marvin."

Everyone laughed.

The class followed Mr. Sullivan into another room with a large table. Microphones on long poles hung from the ceiling. The walls were lined with thickly padded panels. Everyone took a seat around the table.

Mr. Sullivan put on a head set. He spoke through one of the microphones to a man sitting on the other side of a glass window who also had on a headset. "Joe. When you finish the next song, Marvin is going to interview his classmates about the National Day of Prayer. We'll fill in until the winners from the poetry contest arrive. Please have Sally let them in when they arrive. We'll go right into that segment."

"Sounds good," Joe answered.

Mr. Sullivan turned to the students. "When I hold up my hand, you have fifteen seconds to wrap up before we go to a commercial break. If you're talking, quickly finish your thought. You can relax a bit during the commercial. When we're on the air, try not to cough or make any noises because the microphones pick up everything."

Mary's stomach growled loudly. She covered her middle with her arms.

Mr. Sullivan chuckled. "Don't worry. No one will hear that." He turned to Marvin. "Ask questions that you all know the answers to. Then the rest of you can share your thoughts—just like you did in the conference room. Be sure to give your name when you answer a question."

Joe interrupted, "You have thirty seconds until the teaser."

Marvin asked, "What's a teaser?"

"A short introduction to the interview," Mr. Sullivan explained. "After it runs, we'll have another commercial. Then we'll start."

Joe began to count backwards. "Ten, nine, eight, seven, six, five, four, three two, one..."

"This is Randy Sullivan, and you're listening to KXYZ, easy listening radio, inspiring talk. Today we are observing the National Day of Prayer. We have

some young guests from Valley Elementary School
who are going to tell us more about the historical
significance of prayer in our nation. We'll be right
back, so don't go away."

A grocery store ad came over the air. Marvin furiously scribbled some thoughts down on a clean piece of
paper he had gotten from Laura. She slid her notebook
over to help him get more ideas.

Suddenly, Joe began counting backward again.
"Ten, nine, eight, seven, six, five, four, three, two,
one." Everyone took a deep breath.

"This is Randy Sullivan and with me today is a
fifth grade class from Valley Elementary School.

They have been researching the significance of prayer in our nation's history. Marvin Kepple is going to interview his classmates. Are you ready, Marvin?"

"Sure," he responded weakly.

"Then I'll turn the program over to you."

Marvin gulped, then sat straight. His notes shook in his hands. "With me today are eleven of my classmates, our teacher Miss Baker, and our principal Mr. McDonald." His voice sounded shaky at first, then got stronger. "I thought I'd start with this question. Umm. Why did the Pilgrims celebrate the first Thanksgiving?"

As Marvin asked questions about each of their adventures, the students shared what they had learned and what it meant to them. Miss Baker and Mr. McDonald didn't have to help once. Mr. Sullivan kept nodding his head in approval.

After a few moments, the younger children quietly joined them in the studio. The children were dressed in their best, as if their parents had forgotten they were going to be heard, not seen.

After twenty minutes, Mr. Sullivan thanked the fifth grade class and introduced the winners of the contest. The rest of the group listened to the poems as they were read into the microphone. At 4:00, Mr. Sullivan thanked the children and closed the segment. Joe flipped on a CD.

"You were great!" Mr. Sullivan said as he took off his head set. "This was a wonderful program." He turned to Miss Baker's class. "Thanks for helping me out."

"You bet," Marvin responded. "If you ever need a disc jockey, you know where to find me."

"I'll keep that in mind," Mr. Sullivan said sincerely. He led all the children back through the hallway.

Inside the lobby, Mr. Sullivan began talking to Mr. McDonald, Miss Baker and the adults who had brought the younger children. The kids milled around by the outside door.

"Want to meet someone really neat?" Jose asked the younger children.

"How will they see him? He's invisible to everyone except us," Mary asked.

"Don't worry. Kit Cat says all kids can see him. It's just grown-ups who have problems with that."

"Great!" Mary said. "Let's go."

The little kids nodded.

Mary ran to get permission to take them out to the front of the radio station. Then they all rushed out to talk to Kit Cat.

12

I Think We're Going to Win

Jose, Mary and the rest of the fifth grade class led the younger children out of the radio station and to the sidewalk where the bus was parked.

"Kit Cat, where are you?" Jose hollered.

"I hope he's not taking another nap," Elizabeth muttered.

A second grader tugged at Mary's shirt. "Who are we looking for?" he asked.

"Our friend, Kit Cat." Mary pointed to her watch. "He looks like this."

"Ooooh!" The little boy's eyes got as round as saucers.

Just then they heard a voice coming from an unclear direction. "You can't see me; but I can see you."

Marvin's fist punched the air like a general leading the charge. "Let's find him!"

Everyone scrambled around the yard looking for Kit Cat.

Scott shouted, "There he is!" as he pointed to a leafy oak tree that shaded the front of the radio station.

Sure enough, Kit Cat was reclining on a sturdy limb. He grinned. "You finally found me." He grabbed the limb and did a flip like an experienced acrobat. He landed softly onto the plush grass.

The younger children giggled. Several got up enough courage to pet his silky black fur.

The adults began coming out the front door of the station. Kit Cat hugged the little children good-bye. Then he announced, "Fifth graders on the bus!"

Everyone scattered. The Valley Elementary students rushed to their seats; the younger children went to find their parents.

"Where are we going next?" Miss Baker asked as she took her place near the front of the bus.

Kit Cat whirled around in his captain's chair.

"We're going to see how a church and synagogue observe the National Day of Prayer."

Everyone fastened their seat belts as Kit Cat flipped levers and pushed buttons on the control panel. The bus rumbled and growled for a few minutes, then stopped. Everyone on the right side peered out at a wrought iron gate with a sign that read "St. Paul's Methodist Church."

Tony jumped up from his seat. "Hey! My dad's the pastor here."

"Right," Kit Cat said. "Many churches have opened their doors for prayer today. This prayer service is for several churches in the area." He motioned to Tony. "Why don't you lead the way. Mr. McDonald, can you bring them back in thirty minutes? I'll park the bus."

The principal nodded and checked his watch.

Tony led them through the gate and up a path shaded by heavy-limbed trees. They quietly approached the stately old stone church.

A teenager greeted them in the small foyer. She handed each student a brochure called, "A Daily Prayer Guide."[1]

Tony opened the main door into the sanctuary. Several hundred people were either sitting in simple wooden pews or kneeling on red padded cushions around the altar. The sun shone through stained glass windows on the west side. Rays of rainbow light streamed horizontally through the air.

The students entered quietly so they wouldn't disturb the prayerful atmosphere. They found an empty pew at the back and filed in.

A woman rose and read from her Bible:

"If I regard wickedness in my heart, The Lord will not hear; But certainly God has heard; He has given heed to the voice of my prayer. Blessed be God, Who has not turned away my prayer, nor His loving kindness from me. Psalm 66:18-20."

Pastor Nelson, who looked a lot like Tony, stood up at the front. "We will close this time of searching our hearts and confessing our sins and move into a time of praying for our leaders. If you are following the prayer guide, we're on top of the second page."

The class quickly flipped to the right page. They followed along as Pastor Nelson read the instructions. "Pray for the leaders of the country by name, that they might have wisdom, guidance, protection and awareness of God's presence in mind and heart, and that they might practice personal integrity."

"Will someone read 1 Timothy 2:1-2?" he asked.

A middle-aged woman rose from her seat toward the front.

Jose whispered. "That's my mom. Hey, yeah. I remember a flier about this meeting stuck up on our refrigerator. But we go to a Catholic church. I didn't expect her to be here."

Jose's mother read from her Bible.

"I urge that entreaties and prayers, petitions and thanksgiving, be made on behalf of all men, for kings and all who are in authority, in order that we may lead a tranquil and quiet life in all godliness and dignity."

One at a time, people began praying aloud for the President, Vice President, Supreme Court Justices and other leaders. One woman prayed for teachers and principals. Mr. McDonald caught Miss Baker's attention. She smiled back.

Another local minister joined Pastor Nelson at the front. "Now let's pray for those in need," he said. "For prisoners of drugs, alcohol and crime. For prisoners of hunger and illness. Will someone read Matthew 25:37?"

An elderly gentleman stood and read.

"Lord, when did we see You hungry, and feed You, or thirsty, and gave you drink? And when did we see You sick, or in prison, and come to You? And the King will answer and say to them. Truly I say to you, to the extent that you did it to one of these brothers of Mine, even the least of them, you did it to Me."

"Let's pray in our groups," the minister said.

People broke into clusters of two or three and began praying for friends and relatives who were in need. Several Valley Elementary students did, too. Mary prayed for her grandmother who was sick with cancer. George prayed for his uncle who was an alcoholic. Sammy prayed for his brother who had gotten into trouble for stealing baseball cards from the drug store.

"Jesus loves all these people," the minister inter-jected after a few minutes. "And He loves each of us. He came to forgive our sins and to restore our fellowship with God." He broke into a song. "Jesus loves me this I know, for the Bible tells me so."

The congregation joined him. "Little ones to Him belong; They are weak but He is strong."

Tony broke in on the chorus with his strong voice. "Yes, Jesus loves me; Yes, Jesus loves me."

When the song ended, Mr. McDonald looked at his watch. "It's time to go," he whispered. Everyone quietly filed out of the pew, down an aisle, and through the door.

Kit Cat greeted them outside the church. "I thought you might like a snack." He opened a large sack and began to pass out cartons of milk and wrapped cookies.

"Thank you," the students replied eagerly.

"We don't have time to stop and eat," Kit Cat explained. "But you can munch on the way to the synagogue."

Everyone followed Kit Cat back down the path to the main street and left at the end of the sidewalk. Coming to a busy intersection, they waited for the traffic light to turn green. A homeless man with a black garbage bag full of belongings sat near the curb.

Marvin looked down at his unopened milk and the wrapped cookie in his hands. He muttered, "When I was hungry, you fed me." He walked over to the man. "I thought you might like some milk and a cookie."

The man's dirty hand took the food. His voice cracked as he said, "Thank you, son."

The traffic light changed, and the class walked across the street. A block later, they arrived at a building that looked like the hull of a huge ship.

"This is my synagogue," Ben said with a huge smile.

Kit Cat put his arm around Ben. "Then why don't you be the guide?"

Ben's eyes lit up. "Sure."

The group slipped into the building. Although the large ribs of concrete and steel seemed cold from the outside, the inside was warm and pleasant. The group followed Ben across the lobby to a set of glass doors. They peered through the glass at rows of pews filled with men, women and children. At the opposite end of the room, a beautifully carved, dark, wooden structure stood against the wall. Three men and one woman in long black robes sat in chairs on the slightly raised platform.

Ben explained, "That wooden box is the Ark of the Covenant where the Torah, or the Holy Scripture, is kept. See the candelabra with seven candles on each side? That's called the Menorah."

"Are those men pastors?" Tony asked. "They're wearing long robes like my dad does on Sundays."

"They're like pastors," Ben replied. "We call them Rabbis."

Tony's eyes brightened. "I read about Rabbis in the Bible."

Ben pointed to the woman who walked to the right of the platform. "She's a Cantor, or singer. Her voice is really beautiful." He looked back at the others. "Ready to go in?"

Everyone nodded.

"Shalom," greeted a gray-haired woman with a warm smile as they entered. She handed each a book. The cover said *Gates of Prayer: The New Union Prayer Book*. They filed into a pew and turned to page 376 as the woman had directed.

"What's this?" Sammy asked in a surprised voice when he looked at the page.

"It's Hebrew," Ben whispered back. "The service is done in Hebrew and English. Don't worry. You don't have to know the language."

The Rabbi directed everyone to a page in their prayer book that was printed in English. The congregation read the words together.

"Fervently, we invoke Your blessing upon our country and our nation. Enlighten with Your wisdom and sustain with Your power those whom the people have set in authority, the President, his counselors and advisers, the judges, law-givers and executives, and all who are entrusted with our safety and with the guardianship of our rights and our liberties. May peace and good-will obtain among all the inhabitants of our land."[2]

The Rabbi continued with the next section all by himself.

"I will bless the Lord at all times; His praise shall continually be in my mouth. My soul shall make its boast in the Lord; The humble shall hear it and rejoice. O magnify the Lord with me, And let us exalt His name together. I sought the Lord, and he answered me. And delivered me from all my fears."[3]

As the Cantor began to sing a song in Hebrew, the Rabbi opened a door in the Ark of the Covenant. He drew out a large scroll covered in soft green velvet with wooden handles at each end. A glistening silver ornament hung down in front of the Torah.

The Rabbi and Cantor slowly walked up and down the aisle while she continued singing. As they passed, people near them touched their prayer book to the Torah and then to their lips.

Ben whispered, "They're showing respect for the Scripture."

The Rabbi and Cantor returned to the altar and took the velvet covering off the scroll. The Rabbi laid the scroll on the podium. Then the congregation sang a short song in Hebrew.

"That's a blessing upon the reading of the Scripture," Ben explained.

As the Rabbi began to teach on the Ten Commandments, Mr. McDonald motioned that it was time to go. They quietly slipped out.

The class briskly made its way down the block to where Kit Cat had parked the bus. After everyone was seated, Kit Cat revved the engine and maneuvered the bus back to the school.

"I can't believe all the places we went today," Elizabeth told Laura. "The Mayor's Prayer Breakfast, a Governor's Rally, a nursing home, a radio station, and a church and a synagogue."

Laura slipped her prayer guide into her bulging notebook. "I can hardly believe it either. But we sure have a lot of stuff for our essay." She hugged Elizabeth enthusiastically. "And I think we're going to win."

13

The Great Idea

Miss Baker snapped shut her language book. "Okay, it's time," she said.

Her students quickly put away their things. The rustling of papers and plopping of pencils soon quieted. Then the students sat waiting.

"Kit Cat, we're ready," Miss Baker announced.

Kit Cat got up from his chair near the door. He smiled. "This is the part you have to do yourselves. I can't write the essay for you. That wouldn't be fair."

Miss Baker pursed her lips. "I agree. This has to be the students' work." She looked at her class. "What do you think students?" She picked up a piece of chalk and walked to the blackboard. "Call out ideas, and I'll write them down."

"Can't you even help us with ideas?" George asked.

Kit Cat firmly shook his head.

Silence reigned in the classroom. Finally Elizabeth spoke. "Well, it was fun doing the research. But writing the essay. . . That's something else."

"Right" came from all over the classroom.

"How can we write a first-prize essay?" Tony asked. "That's hard."

Miss Baker held out her piece of chalk. "You don't have to start out with a great essay. First we'll just brainstorm ideas. Then, as we go along, the essay will shape up. It just takes a lot of work."

"Yeah, work," Scott muttered.

"I know what," usually shy Laura spoke up. "Let's thank God for the bounty of the land. Like the Pilgrims. We could write an essay on all the things we have to be thankful for in our country."

"Good," Miss Baker said as she printed *PRAY FOR* on the board and *Thank God for the Bounty of Our Land* underneath. "That's a start."

"I think it's more important to remind everyone to pray for our nation's synagogues and churches." Ben said in his slow cautious way. He looked at Tony across the aisle. "Remember that quote under Mrs. Wilson's painting? How did it go? Oh, yeah. Something about America being great because of its churches."

Oknah agreed. "Sure. Who would teach us to pray if we didn't have churches?"

Miss Baker wrote *Our Churches and Synagogues* on the blackboard.

Sammy shook his head. "No, I think we should put the President in our essay. Just think if we didn't have Abraham Lincoln to lead our country during the Civil War." He shook his finger to make his point. "We wouldn't even have a country right now."

Miss Baker listed *Our President* under the other two ideas.

"And what about the Vice President? And the Congressmen and the Supreme Court Justices?" Elizabeth asked. She looked at Sammy. "The President isn't the only one who leads the country."

Miss Baker put those titles under President.

"I say the President only," Jose declared. "Don't forget George Washington. We wouldn't have a country without him either."

"Yeah," Sammy agreed.

Julie put in her two cents. "I think we should pray for those in trouble. Just think about Admiral Lewis when he was a prisoner-of-war. There's a lot of people who need our prayers right now. Let's write about them."

"Like the homeless man," Marvin reminded the class.

Oknah nodded. Her heart went out to anyone who was suffering.

Miss Baker put *People in Need and in Difficult Situations* on the board.

"But what about all the good things God has given our nation?" Laura argued. "Shouldn't we be thankful first?"

"I'm with the churches and synagogues," Tony put in. He gave Ben a high five.

"Well, I think *National* Day of Prayer means praying for our *national* leaders," Elizabeth insisted.

"How about prayer for people in TV and radio?" Scott suggested. "They need prayers too."

Miss Baker wrote *The Media.*

Mary's voice sounded irritated. "I think we should pray for people like Mrs. Wilson. That's what I want to do." She crossed her arms and pouted.

"You got it, Mary," Marvin said smugly.

"What about you, George?" Sammy insisted. "What are you voting for?"

"Well," he said hesitatingly, "What about the Mayor? And State Senator Miller? We met them."

"Hey, yeah," Elizabeth remembered. "I forgot about my uncle. Let's write about prayer for our local *and* national leaders."

Miss Baker put *Local Leaders* next to the national ones.

Suddenly, the room broke into several arguments between the students who wanted to write about leaders, those who voted for churches and synagogues, and the ones who insisted on people in need. Scott sat silently with a scowl on his face. He was the only one who voted for the media.

Miss Baker watched the commotion for a while. She looked at Kit Cat; he shrugged. Clearly, there wasn't one topic that everyone agreed on.

Finally, the voices in the room got too loud. "Quiet!" Miss Baker called. Slowly the noise diminished.

"We have to come to an agreement here," she said softly now that everyone else had stopped talking. "We could take a vote, but I think we could work it out a better way."

The students just looked at their desks. No one spoke for several minutes. Kit Cat sat back in his chair to wait.

Then Laura broke the silence. "Remember what the Continental Congress did when they couldn't agree? They prayed. Well, that's what I've been sitting here doing. I think that's better than arguing."

Heads nodded all over the room. Miss Baker sat behind her desk and bowed her head in private prayer. Some of the students did, too.

Somehow, it seemed as if the feeling in the room began to soften. At first, the change was hardly noticeable. But then, one-by-one, the students' hard looks began to melt into smiles. But still, no one said a word.

Finally, Marvin couldn't stand it any longer. "It's never been this quiet in our room for this long," he said. He had the prayer guide he had gotten on their trip on the top of his desk. He flipped it open as he talked. "Maybe we just can't come up with a good enough idea."

Kit Cat shook his head. "Don't give up yet." He pointed to the board. "You've got a great start."

"Yeah, a good start," Sammy muttered. "But we can't get any farther."

Then Marvin stood up straight as a shot. His face broke out into a huge smile. "I've got it! I've got it!" he shouted.

"What is it?" Miss Baker asked.

"We don't want to write about one thing. We can write about it all."

"But that would make our essay too long," Elizabeth insisted.

"That's not what I mean," Marvin said, excitement raising the pitch on his voice. He waved the prayer guide. "This is what we should do. Let's make a children's prayer guide."

"That's it!" Jose exclaimed. "Our very own prayer guide. We could use it all year round. Other kids could use it, too. We could pass it all over school."

"We could show kids how to pray for synagogues and churches," Ben said.

"And thank God for the bounty of our land," Laura added.

"And put in the media," Scott bellowed.

Normally quiet Oknah pounded her desk. "And pray for the needy."

"All right," Elizabeth agreed. "And put in all our leaders."

Kit Cat broke into his half-moon grin as he saw the excited students plan their essay. "I knew they could do it...with prayer," he said to himself. Then he quietly hopped back into the Klock.

Miss Baker watched him go. She smiled, then went to help her students write a winning essay.

14

We Can Change the Future

Mr. McDonald flew down the hallway of the elementary school. A second grade class that was filing in a line to the cafeteria stopped with their mouths open and watched him go by. Mr. McDonald, the one who was so strict on not running in the halls, was breaking his own rule.

Mr. McDonald put on the brakes when he reached the door to Miss Baker's fifth grade classroom. His slick dress shoes skidded as he anchored himself down. Coming to a stop, he banged his way through the classroom door.

Miss Baker and her students stared at the principal. He was waving a letter with one hand. Holding his heaving chest with the other hand, he managed to gasp, "We...I mean...you won! You all won the contest!"

For a minute, no one moved. Then the meaning of his words hit home.

"We won the essay contest!" Marvin shouted. He stood and twirled in a circle with his hand in the air. "I knew we could do it."

"Let me see," Miss Baker said as she took the letter out of Mr. McDonald's hand. She skimmed the words on the single page. The students all began talking to one another, sounding like a tape cassette that was played too fast, all garbled and noisy.

"Quiet, quiet," Miss Baker demanded. The room got quiet.

"The letter is an invitation to a brunch on the garden patio of the governor's mansion next week. On Tuesday, I'll pass the letter around so you all can see it." She handed it to George who immediately pored over the lines of print. Mary leaned over the aisle to see for herself.

The rest of the day was almost lost for studying. No one could concentrate. Mr. McDonald stayed for an hour, helping the class plan their trip. Miss Baker wrote a big WE WON on the blackboard.

At recess, Kit Cat joined the class as they celebrated their victory. Miss Baker pulled a couple of popcorn packages from a desk drawer and asked Elizabeth to pop them in the microwave in the teacher's lounge. Mr. McDonald sent down cans of soda.

Kit Cat raised his can. The students responded with "Cheers! Cheers!" and "Thanks Kit Cat."

"Can we take your bus to the governor's mansion?" Sammy asked.

Kit Cat shook his head. "I'm sorry, but I won't be making this trip with you."

"What?" Scott demanded. "You deserve to go as much as any of us."

"No," Kit Cat said. "I helped with the research, but you all did the writing."

"Yeah, we did, didn't we?" Marvin said.

Oknah had tears in her eyes. "But it won't be the same without you."

Kit Cat smiled his terrific smile. "Oh yes, it will. You'll have a great time. And you all deserve it." He winked. "I'll be there in spirit." He looked over the class. "There is one piece of unfinished business. I have to take the watches back."

Everyone's face sunk, even Miss Baker's.

Kit Cat walked up and down the aisles, collecting his equipment. When he got to Marvin, Marvin slyly put his watch in his pocket. Kit Cat looked down at Marvin. He gave a tiny smile. Marvin smiled back. Then Kit Cat moved on.

The bell signaled the end of recess. Kit Cat marched to the front of the class. "Got to go."

"Good-bye," everyone hollered.

Kit Cat bowed deeply. "And good-bye to you all." Then he hopped back into the Klock. The second hand ticked away as if Kit Cat had never been there.

Miss Baker slowly turned back to her desk and the pile of homework she had to pass out.

The students could hardly wait until Tuesday. But finally it came. Early that morning, an excited fifth-grade class boarded a Valley Elementary bus for the hour drive to the state capital. They were all dressed in their best.

Marvin took a whole row for himself. He took out his Kit Cat watch. He was secretly doing something to it, but he wouldn't show anyone. Sammy, who was seated behind him, turned around and began talking to Tony. They all ignored Marvin the rest of the trip.

When they got to the capital, an escort took them on a tour of the city in a big charter bus. Two other classes— second and third prize winners—were on the bus, too. Everyone found new friends and talked about how the essay had changed their thinking about their country and prayer.

The bus drove by the main buildings that housed the governmental offices. Miss Baker's fifth graders had the advantage when they reached the Capitol building. The Valley Elementary students had already had a tour during the noon rally on the Capitol steps. They helped the tour guides show the others around.

But the best part was the governor's mansion. The students were escorted by the governor's wife through the mansion. Mrs. Smith was a small, dainty woman. She wore her long skirt and white blouse with a comfortable elegance.

As she took them through the house, she described some of the state history that had taken place in the rooms. She led them to a room that had paintings of early pioneers and native Americans that had helped the territory become a state. Oknah was attracted to the heavily lined face of an Indian chief on the far wall.

Mrs. Smith then guided them through elegant sitting rooms where world famous guests had been entertained. She pointed out an armchair President Lincoln had once sat in when he visited the state.

George poked Jose. "Can't you just see him sitting here?"

"Yeah!" Jose exclaimed.

Mrs. Smith took them to the meeting rooms where history had been made. On one of the walls was a mounted copy of the first page of the State Constitution. Ben tried to speed-read it before the group moved on.

Then they went to the garden patio. It was laid out beautifully. Rows and rows of perfectly trimmed hedges and colorful flower beds ringed the patio. Several long tables with white linen tablecloths were laid out on the copper-red tile. A pool to the left reflected the huge mounds of daisies and mums in wicker baskets on each table and on pedestals placed around the patio.

The students found place cards marked with their names. When they had all taken a seat, Governor Smith led them in a prayer of blessing for the food. Then waiters dressed in flowered shirts and white pants brought out trays of food.

They all ate dozens of Danish rolls, eggs and ham casserole, crepes filled with cherries and blueberries, and freshly sliced pineapple, grapefruit and melons.

When everyone had eaten their fill, the Governor stood behind a small podium. "I'm not hear to make a big speech," he began. "But I do want you to talk about your essays. I've read every one of the winning entries. I'm proud of the scholarship you have all demonstrated."

He held up copies of the three winning essays. "We have classes here from all parts of the state. That makes me feel like the educational system in our state is strong. But more than that, the content of your essays opened my eyes to the importance of praying for our cities, state and nation."

He asked one representative from each class to come and read each essay. The Valley Elementary class was last. They chose Laura to read. Laura squared her shoulders and walked confidently to the podium. She read the short essay in a strong, firm voice.

When she finished, the Governor said, "Those are wonderful essays. Valley Elementary fifth grade class won first prize—not only for the excellent essay they wrote—but also for the prayer guide they included."

The Governor held up a prayer guide. "They helped put feet to their ideas. They have put together a guide that will help children pray for our country."

He handed a stack of prayer guides to one of the waiters. "Please give one to each person," he instructed.

After the guides were passed out to everyone, the Governor went on to tell how prayer had helped him with his responsibilities. He described how he had spent a whole night in prayer during the budget crisis of last year. He told them how he prayed before important sessions of the state senate.

Then Mrs. Smith joined her husband at the podium and told how prayer had helped in her work with drug babies. She described how prayer had helped her cope with the suffering she saw in those little ones. Her love for those babies shone in her eyes.

After she finished, the Governor closed the meeting with a round of applause for the winning classes, one by one. Then the breakfast ended.

Marvin rushed up to the Governor as soon as he could get out of his seat. Several other Valley Elementary students followed him. The Governor asked them about the research they did for their essay. Mary told him about Mrs. Wilson and the nursing home. Jose described the breakfast at the Grand Hotel.

The Governor nodded. "That's great," he said. "You all have put in a lot of work. I can see why your entry was so good."

Just before they turned to leave, Marvin spoke up. "I brought something for you," he said. He pulled out his Kit Cat watch. He looked at it for a moment. Then, with a sly grin, he tapped the crystal like he had seen Kit Cat do when the bus had disappeared. Nothing happened.

Marvin laughed, then handed the watch to the Governor.

The Governor took it. "What's this?"

"It's a Kit Cat watch," Marvin said. He pointed to the crystal where he had printed TIME TO PRAY with a permanent marker.

The Governor smiled. "Yes, this will help remind me to pray all during my busy day. It's just what I need." He strapped it to his wrist, then held it up for everyone to see.

Marvin beamed.

Half an hour later, Miss Baker and her class were on their way home. Everyone was buzzing about all they had seen and heard.

Oknah turned to George in the seat behind her. "Did you think there was anything strange about the Governor's Kit Cat watch?"

George looked at her for a minute. "Yeah," he finally said, "but I was afraid to mention it."

Julie heard their conversation. "Did you see what I saw?"

Oknah nodded. "I think so."

Jose and Sammy leaned over to listen in. So did Laura and Elizabeth. Soon the entire class was involved in the discussion.

"So what did you see?" asked Elizabeth who hated to be in the dark about anything.

Marvin laughed. "It's true. I saw it too. Kit Cat winked at us from the watch just before the Governor's sleeve covered up his face."

The students cheered.

Laura's voice stopped the cheer. "But what about when we get home? Is this it?"

"Of course not," Julie said. "I'm going to use my prayer guide every day. I'm putting it right beside my bed so I will remember every night."

Oknah put her chin on her hands on the seat in front of her. "I made a prayer corner in my bedroom."

"You know what I'm going to do?" Marvin interrupted. "I'm going to write down all my prayers and see how they're answered."

"That sounds like a good idea," Miss Baker said. "We have three weeks of school left. We can use the time to make a list of all our national, state and local leaders. We should find out how we can best pray for each of them. What committees they are on; what responsibilities they have. We can scan the newspaper for events that are happening statewide and in Washington, D.C. Our research is just beginning."

"I think we should give a prayer guide to each person in our school," Mary suggested. "And show them how to use it."

"Good idea," Ben said. "I can hardly wait. Just think, we can help make our future better by praying."

"You bet," Miss Baker said as she sat back to enjoy the rest of the bus ride. "We can change the future for good with prayer."

Your Prayer Guide

How would you like to help change your country's future for good? The National Day of Prayer is for all Americans, no matter what race they are, what they do for a living, or how old they are, or even if they have fur like me. I'm convinced that young people like you have the greatest faith to pray for their country. Prayer doesn't take any special education or skill. It just takes a willing heart.

I know you can pray, too! Let's make a prayer guide just like the one Miss Baker's class used. It will help you remember who to pray for and record how often you pray. You could put it beside your bed, in your desk at school, or any place where you will notice it every day.

To make your prayer guide, take a plain sheet of lined paper. Write DAILY PRAYER GUIDE at the top. Divide the sheet into seven parts. On each part, write the day of the week beginning with Sunday. List the things you should pray for on that day. If you run out of room, use the back of your paper for some of the days. Print or write neatly so it will be easy to read. Your sheet should look something like this:

DAILY PRAYER GUIDE

SUNDAY

Pray for the United States, that its people would seek God.

> Thank God for the bounty of the land.
> Tell God you are sorry for the problems in our nation.
> Ask God to help people be godly and wise.
> Ask God to help people be aware of His love and plan for them.
> Ask God to help you share His love with every one you meet.

MONDAY

Pray for the leaders of our country that they might have wisdom, guidance and protection in leading our nation.

> President
> Vice President
> Supreme Court Justices
> U.S. Ambassadors
> Senators
> Congressmen
> Leaders of our armed forces
> Presidential Cabinet members

TUESDAY

Pray for the leaders of your state, county and city.

Governor	County officials
Lt. Governor	City officials
State Senator	Local judges
State Representative	School authorities
Mayor	

WEDNESDAY

Pray for people in need or in difficult situations.

The homeless and hungry
The ill, those in hospitals or nursing homes
Prisoners and their families
Those hooked on drugs or alcohol
The sad, lonely and friendless

THURSDAY

Pray that those who help people will spread the love of God.

Ministers, priests, rabbis and chaplains
Teachers, social workers, soldiers and scientists
Those who work for newspapers, television,
radio, film industry and magazines
Policemen, firemen and rescue persons
Hospital and nursing home workers

FRIDAY

Pray for people around you and their needs.
 	
    Parents, brothers and sisters
    Grandparents and the elderly
    Relatives and neighbors
    Friends and schoolmates
    Others you meet in your everyday life

SATURDAY

Pray for families in our nation to be places of peace, love, respect and honor
 	
    Ask that parents have wisdom and courage to care for their children.
    Ask that children show respect for others and love and obey their parents.
    Pray for husbands, wives and children of broken homes.
    Pray for those who are trying to put their marriage and homes back together.

Write the names of the President, your Governor, minister, and others beside their titles. Over the next few weeks or months, learn the names of other people you may not know, such as Supreme Court Justices or your local school authorities. Write their names beside their titles.

Keep your list up to date and change the names after an election. On the back of your sheet of paper, make a chart like this:

PRAYER CHART

Use this monthly chart to keep track of the days in which you pray. Put a check mark on each day you remember to pray for your country.

	Week 1	Week 2	Week 3	Week 4
Sunday				
Monday				
Tuesday				
Wednesday				
Thursday				
Friday				
Saturday				

You can make a new Prayer Chart after the month is up. Draw it on a new sheet of paper and tape it over the old one.

You will be surprised at how many charts you will fill up. They will help you keep track of how many months you have been praying for your country. When a year is done, you can make a new prayer guide and begin all over again.

What should you pray for? Pray for specific things that concern you about your country. Maybe your city is having a problem with crime. Or you know of an election being held. Write your prayer requests down so you can review the list later to see how your prayers were answered.

I'm excited about kids praying for our country. I think it will make the difference in our country's future. I think your prayers will help make you a better citizen in the years to come. Think of all the good that will happen when kids begin to pray all over the United States! Together we can change our country's future for good through prayer.

By the President of the United States of America

A Proclamation

Whereas it is the duty of all nations to acknowledge the providence of Almighty God, to obey His will, to be grateful for His benefits, and humbly to implore His protection and favor; and

Whereas both Houses of Congress have, by their joint committee, requested me "to recommend to the people of the United States a day of public thanksgiving and prayer, to be observed by acknowledging with grateful hearts the many and signal favors of Almighty God, especially by affording them an opportunity peaceably to establish a form of government for their safety and happiness."

Now, therefore, I do recommend and assign Thursday, the 26th day of November next, to be devoted by the people of these States to the service of that great and glorious Being who is the beneficent author of all good that was, that is, or that will be; that we may then all unite in rendering unto Him our sincere and humble thanks for His kind care and protection of the people of this country previous to their becoming a nation; for the signal and manifold mercies and the favorable interpositions of His providence in the course and conclusion of the late war; for the great degree of tranquillity, union, and plenty which we have since enjoyed; for the peaceable and rational manner in which we have been enabled to establish constitutions of government for our safety and happiness, and particularly the national one now lately instituted; for the civil and religious liberty with which we are blessed, and the means we have of acquiring and diffusing useful knowledge; and, in general, for all the great and various favors which He has been pleased to confer upon us.

And also that we may then unite in most humbly offering our prayers and supplications to the great Lord and Ruler of Nations, and beseech Him to pardon our national and other transgressions; to enable us all, whether in public or private stations, to perform our several and relative duties properly and punctually; to render our National Government a blessing to all the people by constantly being a Government of wise, just, and constitutional laws, discreetly and faithfully executed and obeyed; to protect and guide all sovereigns and nations (especially such as have shown kindness to us), and to bless them with good governments, peace, and concord; to promote the knowledge and practice of true religion and virtue, and the increase of science among them and us; and, generally, to grant unto all mankind such a degree of temporal prosperity as He alone knows to be best.

Given under my hand, at the city of New York, the 3d day of October, A.D. 1789.

G. WASHINGTON.

A Proclamation

From the President
For a Day of Humiliation, Fasting and Prayer
1863

Whereas, The Senate of the United States, devoutly recognizing the Supreme Authority and Just Government of Almighty God, in all the affairs of men and of nations, has, by a resolution, requested the President to designate and set apart a day for National prayer and humiliation:

And Whereas, It is the duty of nations, as well as of men, to owe their dependence upon the overruling power of God, to confess their sins and transgressions, in humble sorrow, yet with assured hope that genuine repentance will lead to mercy and pardon, and to recognize the sublime truth, announced in the Holy Scriptures and proven by all history, that those nations only are blessed whose God is the Lord:

And, Inasmuch as we know that, by His divine law, nations, like individuals, are subjected to punishments and chastisements in this world, may we not justly fear that the awful calamity of civil war, which now desolates the land, may be but a punishment inflicted upon us for our presumptuous sins, to the needful end of our national reformation as a whole People? We have been the recipients of the choicest bounties of Heaven. We have been preserved these many years in peace and prosperity. We have grown in numbers, wealth, and power as no other nation has ever grown. But we have forgotten God. We have forgotten the gracious hand which preserved us in peace, and multiplied and enriched and strengthened us; and we have vainly imagined, in the deceitfulness of our hearts, that all these blessings were produced by some superior wisdom and virtue of our own. Intoxicated with unbroken success, we have become too self-sufficient to feel the necessity of redeeming and preserving grace, too proud to pray to the God that made us!

It behooves us, then, to humble ourselves before the offended Power, to confess our national sins, and to pray for clemency and forgiveness.

Now, therefore, in compliance with the request, and fully concurring in the views of the Senate, I do, by this my proclamation, designate and set apart THURSDAY, the 30th day of April, 1863, as a day of National Humiliation, Fasting and Prayer. And I do hereby request all the People to abstain on that day from their ordinary secular pursuits, and to unite, at their several places of public worship and their respective homes, in keeping the day holy to the Lord, and devoted to the humble discharge of the religious duties proper to that solemn occasion.

All this being done, in sincerity and truth, let us then rest humbly in the hope, authorized by the Divine teachings, that the united cry of the Nation will be heard on high, and answered with blessings, no less than the pardon of our national sins, and restoration of our now divided and suffering country to its former happy condition of unity and peace.

In Witness Whereof, I have hereunto set my hand, and caused the seal of the United States to be affixed.

By his excellency

ABRAHAM LINCOLN
President of the United States of America

U.S. Senate Report

Calendar No. 1324

82D CONGRESS 2d Session	SENATE	REPORT No. 1389

NATIONAL DAY OF PRAYER

APRIL 2, 1952.—Ordered to be printed

Mr. McCARRAN, from the Committee on the Judiciary, submitted
the following

REPORT

[To accompany H. J. Res. 382]

The Committee on the Judiciary, to which was referred the resolution (H. J. Res. 382) directing the President to proclaim a suitable day each year, other than a Sunday, as a National Day of Prayer, having considered the same, reports favorably thereon, without amendment, and recommends that the resolution do pass.

PURPOSE

The purpose of the proposed legislation is to direct the President to proclaim a National Day of Prayer each year.

STATEMENT

From its beginning the United States of America has been a nation fully cognizant of the value and power of prayer. In the early days of colonization, the Pilgrims frequently engaged in prayer. When the delegates to the Constitutional Convention encountered difficulties in the writing and formation of a Constitution for this Nation, prayer was suggested and became an established practice at succeeding sessions. Today, both Houses of the Congress are opened daily with prayer.

Prayer has indeed been a vital force in the growth and development of this Nation. It would certainly be appropriate if, pursuant to this resolution and the proclamation it urges, the people of this country were to unite in a day of prayer each year, each in accordance with his own religious faith, thus reaffirming in a dramatic manner the deep religious conviction which has prevailed throughout the history of the United States.

Proclamation 2978

NATIONAL DAY OF PRAYER, 1952

WHEREAS from the earliest days of our history our people have been accustomed to turn to Almighty God for help and guidance; and

WHEREAS in times of national crisis when we are striving to strengthen the foundations of peace and security we stand in special need of divine support; and

WHEREAS the Congress, by a joint resolution approved on April 17, 1952 (66 Stat. 64), has provided that the President "shall set aside and proclaim a suitable day each year, other than a Sunday, as a National Day of Prayer, on which the people of the United States may turn to God in prayer and meditation"; and

WHEREAS I deem it fitting that this Day of Prayer coincide with the anniversary of the adoption of the Declaration of Independence, which published to the world this Nation's "firm reliance on the protection of Divine Providence":

NOW, THEREFORE, I, HARRY S. TRUMAN, President of the United States of America, do hereby proclaim Friday, July 4, 1952, as a National Day of Prayer, on which all of us, in our churches, in our homes, and in our hearts, may beseech God to grant us wisdom to know the course which we should follow, and strength and patience to pursue that course steadfastly. May we also give thanks to Him for His constant watchfulness over us in every hour of national prosperity and national peril.

IN WITNESS THEREOF, I have hereunto set my hand and caused the Seal of the United States of America to be affixed.

DONE at the City of Washington this 17th day of June in the year of our Lord nineteen hundred and fifty-two, and of the Independence of the United States of America the one hundred and seventy-sixth.

HARRY S. TRUMAN

Photograph of the National Day of Prayer Signing

May 5, 1988.
Presidential signing of the bill that
established the National Day of Prayer as
the first Thursday of every May.

From left to right: Congressman Tony Hall; Gladys
Harrington; Congressman Frank Wolf; Dr. Jerry Nims;
Vonette Bright; President Ronald Reagan; Pat Boone;
Susan Sorensen; Congressman Carlos Moorhead; Rabbi
Joshua Habermann; Father John O'Connor.

U.S. Department of Justice, Civil Justice Division
Presidential Proclamations 'OK' for Classroom use

The following is an answer to a request by CEAI to Former President Reagan regarding the use of the President's National Day of Prayer Proclamation. Wm. Bradford Reynolds, Assistant Attorney General, Civil Rights Division answers for the President.

This is in response to your letter to the President concerning religious freedom and the school teacher whose principal denied her permission to duplicate and distribute copies of the Presidential Proclamation captioned "National Day of Prayer, 1988." The White House has referred your correspondence to the Department of Justice for a response.

The First Amendment of our Constitution is aimed at promoting, not inhibiting, the free expression of ideas. I can think of no more appropriate place for this principle to be put into practice than in our public schools. While the Supreme Court has barred from the classroom the recitation in unison of a morning prayer, it thankfully has not yet ruled out the starting of each school day with a moment of silence.

Nor is there basis in Supreme Court precedent for forbidding a public school teacher from distributing copies of the President's "National Day of Prayer" proclamation. Neither the freedom of speech nor of religion are served by so tortured a reading of the First Amendment. We have, I would submit, totally lost our constitutional bearings if we surrender to the absurd proposition that public school teachers can be stopped from distributing to students a Presidential Proclamation merely because it has a religious reference point.

As you well know, the concerns you raise are shared by many. Religious freedom is among the most precious guarantees assured us by our forefathers; free speech enjoys equal status. While the courts have in the past placed undue, and at times unconscionable burdens, on the exercise of these freedoms, the more recent judicial trend thankfully appears to be more hospitable to the First Amendment protections.

You should know the President appreciates that you brought this matter to our attention. Thank you for writing.

Sincerely,
Wm. Bradford Reynolds
Assistant Attorney General
Civil Rights Division

S. 1378

One Hundredth Congress of the United States of America

AT THE SECOND SESSION

Begun and held at the City of Washington on Monday, the twenty-fifth day of January,
one thousand nine hundred and eighty-eight

An Act

To provide for setting aside the first Thursday in May as the date on which the
National Day of Prayer is celebrated.

*Be it enacted by the Senate and House of Representatives of the
United States of America in Congress assembled,* That the joint
resolution entitled "Joint Resolution to provide for setting aside an
appropriate day as a National Day of Prayer", approved April 17,
1952 (Public Law 82-324; 66 Stat. 64), is amended by striking "a
suitable day each year, other than a Sunday," and inserting in lieu
thereof "the first Thursday in May in each year".

_____
Speaker of the House of Representatives.

_____
President of the Senate pro tempore.

APPROVED

MAY - 5 1988

Ronald Reagan

[COPY]

155

End Notes

Dear Parents and Teachers

1. Shanker, Albert, "An Essential Part of American History: Teaching About Religion," *New York Times,* Sunday, September 23, 1990.

Chapter 2

1. Purpose for coming to America from the Pilgrims' *Mayflower Compact,* written on November 11, 1620, off Cape Cod. Found in *The History of Plymouth Colony,* modern English edition by William Bradford (New York: Walter J. Black, 1948), p. 100.

Chapter 3

1. From the brochure entitled, "with united hearts..." (Dallas, TX: Thanks-Giving Square Foundation, 1975), p. 5.
2. "with united hearts...", p. 4.
3. Peter Marshall and David Manuel, *The Light and the Glory* (Old Tappen, NJ: Fleming H. Revell Company, 1977), pp. 342, 343.

Chapter 4

1. Adapted from *Faith and Freedom* by Benjamin Hart (Dallas, TX: Lewis and Stanley Publishing Co., 1988), p. 293.

Chapter 5

1. Gary Wills, "The Words That Remade America," *The Atlantic,* June 1992, p. 76. Lincoln's Gettysburg Address was delivered on November 19, 1863, in Gettysburg, Pennsylvania. It is inscribed within the Lincoln Memorial in Washington, D.C.

Chapter 6

1. Reference to Billy Graham's talk in the *House Congressional Record*, February 4, 1952, p. 771, left column.
2. This paragraph of text and the following nine paragraphs are taken from the discussion on the House floor as recorded in the *House Congressional Record*, February 27, 1952, p. 1564.
3. Frederic Fox, "Ups and Downs of the NDP," *University of Princeton Quarterly,* Fall 1972, Number 54, p.11.
4. Fox, "Ups and Downs," p.11.

Chapter 7

1. Eisenhower's suggestion referred to in "Ups and Downs of the NDP," Frederick Fox. *University of Princeton Quarterly,* Fall 1992, Number 54.
2. President Reagan's words are taken from his response to a woman who wrote describing her prayers for him.
3. President George Bush's words were taken verbatim from his 1992 National Day of Prayer Proclamation.

Chapter 8

1. National Day of Prayer bookmark available through the NDP Task Force, P.O Box 15616, Colorado Springs, CO 80935-5616 or call (719)531-3379.
2. Adapted from a quote by Joseph L. Bohart, spokesman for the San Mateo County Community Leader's Prayer Breakfast, *The Times,* Saturday, April 22, 1989.
3. Section inspired by the story of Retired Vice Admiral James B. Stockdale at the San Mateo County Leader's Prayer Breakfast, *The Times,* Saturday, April 22, 1989.

Chapter 9

1. *The Denver Post,* "Entire City Pauses for Prayer Even at the High Tide of Business," January 20, 1905.

2. The National Day of Prayer Task Force compiles a list of observances each year. For more information about what is happening in your area, write P.O. Box 15616, Colorado Springs, CO 80935-5616 or call (719) 531-3379.

Chapter 10

1. Alexis de Tocqueville laid out his research in *Democracy in America*, 1835. The book is an excellent overview of America's beginnings and the influence of religion on its democratic institutions.

Chapter 11

1. Public Service Announcement from the 1989 National Day of Prayer Task Force.

Chapter 12

1. *A Daily Prayer Guide* is available through the National Day of Prayer Task Force, P.O. Box 15616, Colorado Springs, CO 80935-5616 or call (719) 531-3379.
2. *Gates of Prayer: The New Union Prayerbook*, Central Conference of American Rabbis, New York, 1975.
3. Psalms 34:1-4.

About the Authors

Susan Sorensen

Susan Sorensen served as the national coordinator of the National Day of Prayer in 1988 and 1989 and assisted in the passage of the legislation which established the Day as the first Thursday of every May. Susan now coordinates the Michigan Prayer Network under Michigan Family Forum, a family policy council associated with Focus on the Family. She also serves as the Michigan coordinator for the National Day of Prayer Task Force. Many of the current observances of the Day found in this book come from actual observances she has experienced in her work with the National Day of Prayer.

Joette Whims

Joette Whims is Managing Editor for New**Life** Publications, a ministry of Campus Crusade for Christ International. She does writing, editing, curriculum development, video and TV script consulting, and market analysis for editorial projects. She also writes children's curriculum and articles for children's magazines.

Joette has a degree in English literature, including course work in children's and adolescent literature as well as library science. She has worked with children for twenty-five years in many capacities and is the mother of three, ages 5, 12 and 18.

A prayer changes how you feel about life!

WOODY YOUNG is author and co-author of more than 20 books. He is the president of The California Clock Company, manufacturers of the famous Kit-Cat® Klock with its rolling eyes and wagging tail. He is also the creator of the Kit-Cat® Fan Club and the positive character Kit-Cat®, which you see illustrated throughout this book. Some of the Kit-Cat® illustrated book titles you may find in public and school libraries throughout the nation: "ClockWise: How to Tell Time," "MoneyWise"- Introduction to counting money and making change, "SmileWise"- Kit-Cat® cartoons with a message about smiling, "SongWise"- a 4 book series - with each song's background and illustrated for easy learning, and the 100+ series - "100+ Craft & Gift Ideas, "100+ Desserts & Appetizers" and "100+ Party Games"- for all ages and group size. Other very popular Kit-Cat® books are "Our Family Babysitting Guide"- information about the family every sitter needs to know and "So You've Been Asked to Pray"- public prayers for all occasions (the illustrations on this page come from this book). For more information about Kit-Cat® write to Joy Publishing, P.O.Box 827, San Juan Capistrano, CA 92675.

Praying brings out the best in you.